To the best supervisor ever had

To you Rhoda,

thank you

Elie Menassa

The Pattern of Financial Asset Ownership

Wisconsin Individuals, 1949

BY THOMAS R. ATKINSON

A STUDY BY THE
NATIONAL BUREAU OF ECONOMIC RESEARCH, NEW YORK

PUBLISHED BY
PRINCETON UNIVERSITY PRESS, PRINCETON
1956

Copyright © 1956, by Princeton University Press
London: Geoffrey Cumberlege, Oxford University Press
All Rights Reserved

L.C. CARD 56-8387

Printed in the United States of America
by Princeton University Press, Princeton, New Jersey

NATIONAL BUREAU OF ECONOMIC RESEARCH
1956

OFFICERS

Harry Scherman, *Chairman*
Gottfried Haberler, *President*
George B. Roberts, *Vice-President and Treasurer*
W. J. Carson, *Executive Director*

DIRECTORS AT LARGE

Wallace J. Campbell, *Director, Cooperative League of the USA*
Solomon Fabricant, *New York University*
Albert J. Hettinger, Jr., *Lazard Frères and Company*
Oswald W. Knauth, *Beaufort, South Carolina*
H. W. Laidler, *Executive Director, League for Industrial Democracy*
Shepard Morgan, *Norfolk, Connecticut*
George B. Roberts, *Vice-President, The First National City Bank of New York*
Beardsley Ruml, *New York City*
Harry Scherman, *Chairman, Book-of-the-Month Club*
George Soule, *Bennington College*
N. I. Stone, *Consulting Economist*
J. Raymond Walsh, *New York City*
Joseph H. Willits, *Director, The Educational Survey, University of Pennsylvania*
Leo Wolman, *Columbia University*
Donald B. Woodward, *Vick Chemical Company*
Theodore O. Yntema, *Vice-President–Finance, Ford Motor Company*

DIRECTORS BY UNIVERSITY APPOINTMENT

E. Wight Bakke, *Yale*
Arthur F. Burns, *Columbia*
Melvin G. de Chazeau, *Cornell*
G. A. Elliott, *Toronto*
Frank W. Fetter, *Northwestern*
H. M. Groves, *Wisconsin*

Gottfried Haberler, *Harvard*
Clarence Heer, *North Carolina*
R. L. Kozelka, *Minnesota*
C. Arthur Kulp, *Pennsylvania*
T. W. Schultz, *Chicago*
Jacob Viner, *Princeton*

DIRECTORS APPOINTED BY OTHER ORGANIZATIONS

Percival F. Brundage, *American Institute of Accountants*
Harold G. Halcrow, *American Farm Economic Association*
S. H. Ruttenberg, *Congress of Industrial Organizations*
Murray Shields, *American Management Association*
Boris Shishkin, *American Federation of Labor*
W. Allen Wallis, *American Statistical Association*
John H. Williams, *American Economic Association*
Harold F. Williamson, *Economic History Association*

RESEARCH STAFF

Solomon Fabricant, *Director of Research*
Geoffrey H. Moore, *Associate Director of Research*

Moses Abramovitz
Morris A. Copeland
David Durand
Milton Friedman
Raymond W. Goldsmith
Millard Hastay
W. Braddock Hickman
Daniel M. Holland
Thor Hultgren

John W. Kendrick
Simon Kuznets
Clarence D. Long
Ruth P. Mack
Ilse Mintz
G. Warren Nutter
Lawrence H. Seltzer
George J. Stigler
Leo Wolman

Herbert B. Woolley

RELATION OF THE DIRECTORS
TO THE WORK AND PUBLICATIONS
OF THE NATIONAL BUREAU OF ECONOMIC RESEARCH

1. The object of the National Bureau of Economic Research is to ascertain and to present to the public important economic facts and their interpretation in a scientific and impartial manner. The Board of Directors is charged with the responsibility of ensuring that the work of the National Bureau is carried on in strict conformity with this object.
2. To this end the Board of Directors shall appoint one or more Directors of Research.
3. The Director or Directors of Research shall submit to the members of the Board, or to its Executive Committee, for their formal adoption, all specific proposals concerning researches to be instituted.
4. No report shall be published until the Director or Directors of Research shall have submitted to the Board a summary drawing attention to the character of the data and their utilization in the report, the nature and treatment of the problems involved, the main conclusions and such other information as in their opinion would serve to determine the suitability of the report for publication in accordance with the principles of the National Bureau.
5. A copy of any manuscript proposed for publication shall also be submitted to each member of the Board. For each manuscript to be so submitted a special committee shall be appointed by the President, or at his designation by the Executive Director, consisting of three Directors selected as nearly as may be one from each general division of the Board. The names of the special manuscript committee shall be stated to each Director when the summary and report described in paragraph (4) are sent to him. It shall be the duty of each member of the committee to read the manuscript. If each member of the special committee signifies his approval within thirty days, the manuscript may be published. If each member of the special committee has not signified his approval within thirty days of the transmittal of the report and manuscript, the Director of Research shall then notify each member of the Board, requesting approval or disapproval of publication, and thirty additional days shall be granted for this purpose. The manuscript shall then not be published unless at least a majority of the entire Board and a two-thirds majority of those members of the Board who shall have voted on the proposal within the time fixed for the receipt of votes on the publication proposed shall have approved.
6. No manuscript may be published, though approved by each member of the special committee, until forty-five days have elapsed from the transmittal of the summary and report. The interval is allowed for the receipt of any memorandum of dissent or reservation, together with a brief statement of his reasons, that any member may wish to express; and such memorandum of dissent or reservation shall be published with the manuscript if he so desires. Publication does not, however, imply that each member of the Board has read the manuscript, or that either members of the Board in general, or of the special committee, have passed upon its validity in every detail.
7. A copy of this resolution shall, unless otherwise determined by the Board, be printed in each copy of every National Bureau book.

(Resolution adopted October 25, 1926 and revised February 6, 1933 and February 24, 1941)

NATIONAL BUREAU OF ECONOMIC RESEARCH

Committee on Research in Finance

In the planning and conduct of its studies in finance the National Bureau benefits from the advice and guidance of its Committee on Research in Finance.

The members of the Committee are:

RALPH A. YOUNG, Chairman—*Director, Division of Research and Statistics, Board of Governors of the Federal Reserve System*
WILLIAM J. CARSON, Secretary—*University of Pennsylvania; Executive Director, National Bureau of Economic Research*
BENJAMIN HAGGOTT BECKHART—*Columbia University*
GEORGE W. COLEMAN—*Economist, Mercantile Trust Company*
EDISON H. CRAMER—*Chief, Division of Research and Statistics, Federal Deposit Insurance Corporation*
ERNEST M. FISHER—*Columbia University*
F. CYRIL JAMES—*Principal and Vice-Chancellor, McGill University*
WALTER LICHTENSTEIN—*Vice-President (retired), First National Bank of Chicago*
WALTER MITCHELL, JR.
SHEPARD MORGAN
WILLIAM I. MYERS—*Dean, College of Agriculture, Cornell University*
JAMES J. O'LEARY—*Director of Investment Research, Life Insurance Association of America*
GEORGE B. ROBERTS—*Vice-President, The First National City Bank of New York; Vice-President and Treasurer, National Bureau of Economic Research*
HAROLD V. ROELSE—*Vice-President, Federal Reserve Bank of New York*
R. J. SAULNIER—*Council of Economic Advisers*
CASIMIR A. SIENKIEWICZ—*President, Central-Penn National Bank of Philadelphia*
WOODLIEF THOMAS—*Economic Adviser, Board of Governors of the Federal Reserve System*
DONALD S. THOMPSON—*First Vice-President, Federal Reserve Bank of Cleveland*
JOHN H. WILLIAMS—*Nathaniel Ropes Professor of Political Economy, Harvard University; Economic Adviser, Federal Reserve Bank of New York*
JOHN H. WILLS—*Vice-President and Economist, Northern Trust Company*
LEO WOLMAN—*Columbia University; Research Staff, National Bureau of Economic Research*
DONALD B. WOODWARD—*Chairman, Finance Committee, Vick Chemical Company*

Foreword

As the title of this report states, the statistical data presented and analyzed herein relate to a single year, 1949, and to a single state, Wisconsin. These limitations on the study's scope are, of course, unfortunate. But while the limitations will be obvious to the reader when he picks up the book, it will be no less obvious to him when he puts it down that some remarkable contributions to our understanding of the factors affecting the ownership of stocks and bonds and other financial assets have been made. Indeed, it will become apparent that many of the results could not possibly be peculiar to a single year or to a single state. Most of them are so plausible that the reader is likely to fall into a trap, and forget that he is reading about Wisconsin, 1949. I hope that all readers will manage to avoid the trap. More than that, I hope that some will be sufficiently impressed by the prospects uncovered by Atkinson's exploration to start further investigations that will refute or verify the findings, and thereby lift some of them, at least, to the plane of generalization. If this book fathers such a train of consequences its contribution will indeed be great.

The study was completed under a collaborative agreement between the University of Wisconsin and the National Bureau of Economic Research. As Atkinson points out in his personal acknowledgments, assistance was obtained in the planning and execution of his study from associates at the University of Wisconsin; in addition, a grant of funds from the University of Wisconsin Research Committee sufficed to cover the major part of the clerical and related expenses involved in transcribing and processing data from individual tax returns. As an additional contribution, the University made available its machine tabulating and computing services.

Over the major part of the study's duration, Atkinson held an appointment as a research associate at the National Bureau under a grant from the Carnegie Corporation of New York.

It is a pleasure to record the satisfaction of the National Bureau with the success of this collaborative arrangement and to express our gratitude for the help of the several parties who made it possible.

R. J. SAULNIER
Director, Financial Research Program

March 1955

Acknowledgments

This study was begun as a doctoral dissertation at the University of Wisconsin and carried out as a joint research project under the sponsorship of the National Bureau of Economic Research and the University of Wisconsin. The author is deeply indebted to the Carnegie Corporation for his appointment as a research associate with the National Bureau and to the Bureau itself for an interim staff appointment which made the study possible. Appreciation is gladly acknowledged, also, to the University of Wisconsin, for providing funds for clerical help and making available the resources of the University in the preparation of the materials. The data on which this study is based were compiled in early 1950 with the cooperation, for which we are most grateful, of the Department of Taxation of the State of Wisconsin.

Professor James S. Earley of the University of Wisconsin played a crucial role both in planning the study and in guiding its execution. To Raymond J. Saulnier, Director of the Financial Research Program of the National Bureau, great credit is due for advice on the form and type of questions with which the study deals. Geoffrey H. Moore, Associate Director of Research, and David Durand, both of the National Bureau, have been instrumental in providing insights into many of the problems which were encountered. In the early stages of the study, the assistance of Professor W. D. Knight of the Bureau of Business Research of the University of Wisconsin and Arthur E. Wegner, then Commissioner of Taxation of Wisconsin, was of the utmost importance and is deeply appreciated. Without their help as well as the wholehearted cooperation of the local Assessors of Income and their staffs, this study would not have been possible. I am also indebted to Professors Frank Graner, Harold M. Groves, and Harold G. Fraine of the University of Wisconsin and to Daniel A. Kerth of Robert W. Baird and Company for frequent advice on specific problems. Professor Lawrence R. Klein of the University of Michigan and Raymond W. Goldsmith made many useful comments on the manuscript.

It may be truthfully said that without the helpful cooperation and assistance of the Computing Service of the University of Wisconsin this study would not have been possible. The enormous job of processing the mass of data was possible only by use of the mechanical tabulating equipment made available by this or-

ACKNOWLEDGMENTS

ganization. To Professor Kenneth J. Arnold and Fred Gruenberger, therefore, I acknowledge a considerable debt. Martha S. Jones of the National Bureau has also been helpful in this respect. Finally, credit is due to Mary Detrick, Caroline Evans, Marshall Schwid, and to Sue Atkinson, my wife, for the important role they played in preparing the original material for tabulation; to Catherine P. Martin for statistical assistance; to Mildred E. Courtney, who supervised the typing; to H. Irving Forman, who drew the charts; and to Mary Phelps for helpful editing.

In the final analysis, the success of a project of this type depends on the willingness of many individuals to provide assistance and cooperation in undertakings that go far beyond their normal procedures. The completion of this study testifies to the actual practicability of doing basic research in the social sciences even where a high degree of functional and administrative specialization would seem to preclude such studies.

THOMAS R. ATKINSON

March 1955

Contents

FOREWORD	ix
ACKNOWLEDGMENTS	xi
1. SUMMARY OF FINDINGS	3
Source of Data	8
The Relation of Income to Asset Holdings	11
The Relation of Occupation and City Size to Type of Asset Holding	13
Characteristics of Traded Stock Holdings	16
Suggested Areas for Further Research	22
2. FINANCIAL ASSET OWNERSHIP AND THE FLOW OF SAVINGS AND INVESTMENT	25
The Sources of Saving	28
The Flow of Personal Savings into Investment	31
Summary	38
3. USE OF WISCONSIN TAX RETURNS FOR ESTIMATES OF ASSET HOLDINGS	40
The Sample	40
Method of Valuing Asset Holdings	46
Time Deposits and Related Claims	46
Direct Debt Assets (bonds, notes, etc.)	47
Corporate Stocks	48
Traded stocks	49
Untraded stocks	50
Coverage of the Survey	53
4. THE RELATION BETWEEN INCOME STATUS AND THE PATTERN OF INVESTMENT	58
The Relation between Income and Financial Asset Ownership	60
Frequency of Ownership	60
Size of Holdings	65

xiii

CONTENTS

    Comprehensive Measures of Financial Asset Ownership   68
        Composition of Financial Asset Holdings   68
        The Distribution of Financial Assets   74
        Cause and Effect   78

5. THE EFFECTS OF OCCUPATION AND CITY SIZE ON INVESTMENT IN FINANCIAL ASSETS   86
    Occupation   87
        Ownership of Business Interest Stocks   96
    Size of City   98
        Localization of Investment   103

6. THE CHARACTERISTICS OF TRADED STOCK HOLDINGS   108
    The Markets in Which Stocks Are Traded   109
    Preferred versus Common Issues   112
    Industry of Stocks Held   114
    Risk Rating of Stock Holdings   119
    Diversification   125
    Yield   128
    Average Turnover of Holdings   131
    Price per Share   134
    Summary   138

APPENDIX A. Tables   141

APPENDIX B. Wisconsin Income Tax Returns   163

INDEX   175

Tables

1. Comparative Saving by Income and Occupational Groups of Spending Units in the United States, 1949 — 30
2. Sources and Uses of Net New Investment Funds of the Personal Sector, 1949 — 33
3. Proportion of Spending Units in the United States Reporting Various Types of Additions to or Withdrawals from Savings, 1949 — 34
4. Distribution of Average Net Change in Total Assets by Type of Asset, for Income Groups of Urban Spending Units in the United States, 1941 — 36
5. Estimated Amount of Financial Assets Held by Individuals and Unincorporated Business Firms in the United States, 1949 — 38
6. Derivation of Blow-up Factors for Estimating Asset Holdings of Wisconsin Individuals from Sampled Tax Returns — 45
7. Estimated Frequency of Ownership of Specified Types of Financial Asset by Wisconsin Individuals, 1949 — 61
8. Composition of Financial Asset Holdings for Income Groups of Wisconsin Individuals, 1949 — 69
9. Composition of Holdings of Time Deposits and Related Claims for Income Groups of Wisconsin Individuals, 1949 — 69
10. Composition of Direct Debt Asset Holdings for Income Groups of Wisconsin Individuals, 1949 — 70
11. Composition of Corporate Equity Asset Holdings for Income Groups of Wisconsin Individuals, 1949 — 70
12. Composition of Asset Holdings for Harvard Sample of Individual Investors Grouped by Income, 1949 — 72
13. Estimated Distributions of Value of Checking Accounts, U.S. Savings Bonds, and Life Insurance Premium Payments in the United States, 1950, by Income Group — 76
14. Estimated Distribution of the Value of Traded or Marketable Stocks by Income Group: Three Surveys Compared — 77
15. Relative Importance of Reported Components of Income for Income Groups of Wisconsin Individuals Having Financial Assets, 1949 — 78
16. Actual and Hypothetical Yields from Financial Asset Holdings of Wisconsin Individuals Grouped by Income, 1949 — 79
17. Composition of Asset Holdings for Harvard Sample of Individual Investors Grouped by Wealth, 1949 — 81
18. Frequency of Ownership of Liquid Assets and of Corporate Stock for Occupational Groups of Spending Units in the United States, Early 1949 — 89

CONTENTS

19. Estimated Distributions of Value of Checking Accounts, U.S. Savings Bonds, and Life Insurance Premium Payments in the United States, 1950, by Occupational Group   92
20. Composition of Financial Asset Holdings of Wisconsin Individuals Grouped by Occupation within Income Group, 1949   95
21. Relative Importance of Business Interest Stock in Holdings of Traded and of Untraded Stock for Income Groups of Wisconsin Individuals, 1949   97
22. Frequency of Ownership of Liquid Assets and of Corporate Stock for Community Size Groups of Spending Units in the United States, Early 1949   99
23. Composition of Financial Asset Holdings for Wisconsin Individuals Grouped by Size of Community within Income Group, 1949   103
24. Distribution of Traded Stock Holdings by Location of Operations of Issuing Corporation, for Income Groups of Wisconsin Individuals, 1949   105
25. Estimated Turnover of Stocks Traded in Specified Markets and of Untraded Stocks, 1949   111
26. Distribution of Traded Stock Holdings According to Market in Which Stock is Traded, for Income Groups of Wisconsin Individuals, 1949   112
27. Distribution of Traded and of Untraded Stock Holdings between Preferred and Common Issues, for Income Groups of Wisconsin Individuals, 1949   114
28. Distribution of Untraded Stock Holdings by Industry of Issuing Corporation, for Income Groups of Wisconsin Individuals, 1949   118
29. Relation of Average Number of Issues Held, and of Percentage of Holders with Only One Issue, to Income Level and Size of Holding for Wisconsin Individuals Owning Traded Stock, 1949   127
30. Yields of Traded and of Untraded Stock Held, for Income Groups of Wisconsin Individuals, 1949   131
31. Estimated Turnover of Traded Stock Holdings for Income Groups of Wisconsin Individuals, 1949   132
32. Distribution of Traded Stock Holdings Sold in 1949 by Length of Time Held, for Income Groups of Wisconsin Individuals   133

A-1. Estimated Amount of Interest and Dividend Income from Financial Asset Holdings of Wisconsin Individuals, by Income of Recipient and Type of Asset, 1949   141
A-2. Derivation of Market Value Equivalent for Untraded Stock Held by Income Groups of Wisconsin Individuals, 1949   142

CONTENTS

A-3. Estimated Value of Financial Asset Holdings of Wisconsin Individuals, by Income of Holder and Type of Asset, 1949 — 143

A-4. Estimated Value of Specified Types of Financial Asset Held by Wisconsin Individuals, and Estimated Number of Holders of Some Such Asset, by Size of Holdings and Income of Holder, 1949 — 144

A-5. Estimated Number of Wisconsin Individuals Holding Specified Types of Financial Asset, by Income of Holder, 1949 — 146

A-6. Estimated Mean and Median Size of Holdings for Specified Types of Financial Asset Held by Wisconsin Individuals, 1949, by Income of Holder — 147

A-7. Estimated Number of Wisconsin Individuals Holding Specified Types of Financial Asset, by Occupation and Income of Holder, 1949 — 148

A-8. Estimated Value of Specified Types of Financial Asset Holdings of Wisconsin Individuals, by Occupation and Income of Holder, 1949 — 149

A-9. Estimated Number of Wisconsin Individuals Holding Specified Types of Financial Asset, by Size of Community and Income of Holder, 1949 — 151

A-10. Estimated Value of Specified Types of Financial Asset Holdings of Wisconsin Individuals, by Size of Community and Income of Holder, 1949 — 152

A-11. Estimated Dividends from Traded and from Untraded Stocks, and Value of Holdings, for Income Groups of Wisconsin Individuals, 1949 — 154

A-12. Industrial Classification of Traded Stock Holdings of Wisconsin Individuals, by Income of Holder, 1949 — 155

A-13. Industrial Classification of Untraded Stock Holdings of Wisconsin Individuals, by Income of Holder, 1949 — 157

A-14. Estimated Value of Rated Stock Holdings of Wisconsin Individuals, by Income of Holder and Grade of Stock, 1949 — 158

A-15. Risk Position of Wisconsin Individuals Holding Rated Stock, by Income of Holder, 1949 — 159

A-16. Estimated Value of Traded Stock Sold by Wisconsin Individuals, by Income of Holder and Length of Time Held, 1949 — 160

A-17. Estimated Distribution of Wisconsin Individuals Holding Traded Stock, by Average Price Per Share Held and Income of Holder, 1949 — 161

Charts

1. Estimated Frequency of Ownership of Specified Types of Financial Asset, 1949, for Income Groups of Wisconsin Individuals — 63
2. Estimated Frequency of Ownership of Specified Types of Financial Asset, for Income Groups of Spending Units in the United States — 64
3. Median Size of Holdings of Specified Types of Financial Asset, 1949, for Income Groups of Wisconsin Individuals — 66
4. Estimated Median Size of Holdings of Specified Types of Financial Asset, for Income Groups of Spending Units in the United States — 67
5. Income Distribution of the Population and of Specified Types of Financial Asset Holdings of Wisconsin Individuals, 1949 — 75
6. Composition of Financial Asset Holdings for Wisconsin Individuals Grouped by Size of Holdings within Income Group, 1949 — 82
7. Occupational Distribution of the Population, and of Financial Asset Ownership by Wisconsin Individuals in 1949 — 90
8. Composition of Financial Asset Holdings for Occupational Groups of Wisconsin Individuals, 1949 — 93
9. Community Size Distribution of the Population and of Financial Asset Ownership by Individuals in Wisconsin, 1949 — 101
10. Composition of Financial Asset Holdings for Community Size Groups of Wisconsin Individuals, 1949 — 102
11. Relative Importance of Stocks of Selected Industries in the Traded Stock Holdings of Income Groups of Wisconsin Individuals, 1949 — 115-116
12. Distribution of Stockholdings by Fitch Agency Rating, 1949, for Income Groups of Wisconsin Individuals — 121
13. Relationship between Income Level and Quality of Holdings for Wisconsin Individuals Owning Traded Stock, 1949 — 123
14. Relationship between Income Level and Risk Position for Wisconsin Individuals Grouped by Size of Holding of Traded Stocks, 1949 — 124
15. Distribution of Holders of Rated Stock by Risk Position, for Income Groups of Wisconsin Individuals, 1949 — 126
16. Relationship between the Quality and Yield of Rated Stock Holdings of Wisconsin Individuals, 1949 — 129
17. Distribution of Holders of Traded Stock by Average Price per Share of Their Holdings, 1949, for Income Groups of Wisconsin Individuals — 135
18. Relationship between Income Level of Holder and Price per Share of Wisconsin Individuals' Holdings, 1949, for Stocks of Different Rating Grade — 137

The Pattern of Financial Asset Ownership

WISCONSIN INDIVIDUALS, 1949

CHAPTER 1

Summary of Findings

THIS study of financial asset ownership lies astride two broad areas of research. On the one hand, the nature of most of the data analyzed is such as to classify the study with many other studies of distributions of income and wealth. Financial assets, bonds, stocks, bank accounts, and the like, are a component of the wealth possessed by individuals,[1] and the distribution of such assets among income groups, wealth groups, occupational groups, and city size groups provides insight into the distribution of wealth in general. Financial assets are also income-earning assets, so that their distribution among the population inevitably determines a part of the distribution of total income.

On the other hand, financial assets are not only a component of wealth but they are the visible evidence or "tracks" of flows of investment funds, ancient and distorted or new and fresh, as the case may be. Hence the distribution of financial assets among income groups tells us something about the source of investment funds derived from individual savings. Moreover, differences in the composition of financial assets held by different income, wealth, occupational, and city size groups tell us something about the important variables affecting the flow of funds into debt or equity investment, and how changes in these variables arising from changes in the economic and social structure may be expected to affect the flow of funds from individuals into particular types of investment. It may be of interest, before summarizing major findings in some detail, to indicate briefly how they relate to recent developments in each of the broad areas concerned.

The study was not directed specifically to the problem of preparing or investigating distributions of income and wealth. Naturally, however, our data show the distribution of particular types of wealth by income strata of the population as well as by stratifications related to occupation and city size. Perhaps the most sig-

[1] Throughout the report the term "individual" will be used in a generic sense to distinguish natural persons from institutions, such as business firms, fiduciaries, and nonprofit organizations. Strict accuracy in that usage, to be sure, is impossible because much of the material is derived from sources which do not allow the separation of proprietors' personal accounts from those of their businesses. In any case, it is not meant to use the term individual to distinguish single persons from families of two or more.

SUMMARY OF FINDINGS

nificant findings in this area relate to the effect of the distribution of investment assets upon the distribution of income at any particular moment. Here the study follows the path pointed out by Milton Friedman in attempting to analyze the reasons for an observed distribution of income rather than attempting to develop the distributions themselves.[2] Broadly speaking, the study shows that groups of individuals with higher incomes and assets hold a greater proportion of their financial assets in corporate stocks, which are normally high paying as compared with debt assets and deposit claims. The result is that the distribution of income is affected not only by the gross distribution of wealth but by the effect of income and wealth status upon the types of assets chosen by different income groups *and* by the differences in yields of the various major types of financial assets. In addition, holders of stocks who have some degree of control of the issuing corporation in many cases receive salary income whose size may be affected by that control. There is a complicated interaction, in other words, between income and wealth distributions so far as the effect of investment income upon those distributions is concerned. This evidence appears to confirm the findings of Morris A. Copeland.[3]

The emphasis of the study has been less on providing analytical insight into distributions of income and wealth, and more on providing insight into the flow of funds. In language which perhaps oversimplifies the problems involved, attention is on the *stocks* of accumulated financial assets for what they tell us about the *flow* of individual savings into investment through financial institutions or as direct debt assets or as corporate equity assets.

Much concern has been expressed in recent financial literature over the relation between the present distribution of income and the ability of the economy to generate funds for equity as distinct from debt investment. As an economy moves toward greater equality in the distribution of income, one hypothesis goes, not only is aggregate personal saving reduced but a greater share of it is done by the lower and medium income groups, who might be expected to prefer institutional and debt forms of financial investment over equity outlets for their savings. Should the level of total personal income remain unchanged, nevertheless a reduction

---

[2] Milton Friedman, comment in *Conference on Research in Income and Wealth, Volume Thirteen* (National Bureau of Economic Research, 1951), pp. 55-60.

[3] Morris A. Copeland, "The Social and Economic Determinants of the Distribution of Income in the United States," *American Economic Review*, Vol. XXXVII, No. 1 (March 1947), pp. 57-75.

SUMMARY OF FINDINGS

in the flow of funds for investment in equities would be expected to result from the changed income distribution. In part the verisimilitude of this and related hypotheses depends upon the existence of particular patterns of investment preference that are associated with the income level of the individual. The assumed preference in the low and medium income groups is for debt assets and institutional forms of investment, and in the upper income groups for equity assets.

Although a considerable part of present thinking on finance seems to be based upon the belief that such patterns of investment preference do exist, little attention has been paid to the phenomenon itself. Instead economic literature seems almost entirely concerned with developing the ramifications of such investment patterns. The present study is an attempt to set forth what is known about the pattern of investment preferences. It leaves to others the formulation of the implications of such a pattern.

The analysis deals almost entirely with the supply side of the equity capital problem. We find evidence from analyzing the types of financial assets held by individuals in different income ranges that the lower income groups are the major suppliers of funds in debt form—either directly, through bonds, mortgages, etc., or indirectly, through deposits held by financial intermediaries. The upper income groups, on the other hand, are the major suppliers of corporate equity funds.

This difference in the source of the bulk of equity as against debt funds is a result of two influences. First, as financial asset data are viewed from low to progressively higher income groups, the proportion of individuals holding corporate equity assets is found to increase sharply—more so than the proportions holding debt and deposit types of asset. Second, the median size of equity asset holdings increases, more than is the case with debt or deposit assets. These two influences—frequency of ownership and size of holding—undoubtedly reflect, at least in part, attitudinal differences in individuals of different economic status. The result appears to be that savings originating in the low and medium income groups tend to find quite different outlets than savings originating in high income groups. These findings tend to confirm the speculations of many persons as to the different forms taken by savings arising in the lower as contrasted with the higher income groups.

SUMMARY OF FINDINGS

The question whether the supply of equity capital is now, or has ever been, deficient is not considered because the problem of the necessary amount of new equity capital is not examined in this study, even though some of the most challenging questions in the field of finance lie in that area. For example, what is the effect of a progressive income tax on the supply of venture capital? Have we gone so far toward equality of income distribution that the possibility of stabilizing the economy at a high level of employment and output is threatened by an insufficiency of investment funds in appropriate form? Does the tax-exempt privilege of state and local government bonds draw the savings of high income individuals from equity investment? Should financial intermediaries be allowed to increase their investments in equities to offset the alleged drying-up of the accustomed source of such funds? These questions are beyond the scope of the present investigation, but no one of them can be answered adequately without a knowledge of the investment preference patterns of individuals and how they are related to income levels.[4]

Simon Kuznets points out that there is strong evidence of cyclical shifts in the proportion of total savings accounted for by the upper income groups. He then raises the question of the implications of such shifts for the economy if individuals at different income levels tend to have relatively set patterns of investment.[5]

[4] For examples of problems in connection with which individual investment patterns at different income levels are deemed important, see the following: New York Stock Exchange, *Economic Progress: Tax Revision and the Capital Market* (New York, October 1947); National Association of Manufacturers, *Capital Formation under Free Enterprise* (New York, October 1948); Harry G. Guthmann, "The Movement of Debt to Institutions and Its Implication for the Interest Rate," *Journal of Finance*, March 1950, pp. 70-87; Paul L. Howell, "The Effects of Federal Income Taxation on the Form of External Financing by Business," and discussion by M. D. Ketchum, *Journal of Finance*, September 1949, pp. 208-26; C. R. Noyes, "The Prospect for Economic Growth," *American Economic Review*, March 1947, pp. 13-33.

[5] Kuznets finds that the saving-income ratio for the upper income groups remains relatively stable, and that because the share of the top 5 per cent of income recipients in total income usually moves counter to the cycle, the share of the upper income group in total individual saving must be higher in depression than in prosperity. (See his *Shares of Upper Income Groups in Income and Savings*, National Bureau of Economic Research, Occasional Paper 35, 1950.) If then the preference of the upper income groups for equity investment and that of the lower income groups for investment in the form of debt assets and deposit claims are maintained relatively unchanged throughout the cycle, it follows that the proportion of savings seeking equity investment would tend to be greater in depressions than in boom times.

Whether and in what manner this tendency works itself out depends on how strictly the patterns hold in the face of changes in stock prices, interest rates, etc. This range of questions goes far beyond the scope of the present study.

The present study tends to show the presence of patterns of savings allocation characteristic of particular income groups. Cyclical changes in the proportion of saving accounted for by different income strata of the population would seem to react upon these patterns and produce variations in the proportion of individual financial investment taking debt versus equity form. Further research is needed to determine whether investment patterns are, in fact, relatively constant or whether they also vary over the cycle.

One of the major findings of the study is that the ownership of closely held or seldom traded corporate issues is enormously important in the total equity capital picture and is to a very great degree concentrated in the topmost income groups. Moreover, it is largely concentrated with individuals who receive wages or salaries from the issuing corporation; such persons hold nearly two-thirds of the total value of untraded stock. This finding lends credence to the belief that one of the real problems of small and growing businesses is that of obtaining funds without diminution of control over the corporation, a problem mentioned in nearly all studies of small business finance. A related finding is that investors tend to prefer local stocks (when available on comparable terms) over stocks of corporations located at a distance.

The last chapter of the report deals with the characteristics of the publicly traded stocks held by individuals and how they differ as between income groups. Here the study confronts certain institutional aspects of the marketing and transfer of corporate ownership. It analyzes the relation of income level to holdings of common versus preferred stocks, to stocks traded in various markets, yields of stocks, industry, degree of diversification, turnover, and price per share. Accordingly, the analysis is supplementary to recent studies of stocks and stock ownership.[6]

The subject of individual attitudes toward risk taking is taken up directly. There have been a number of theoretical discussions of the role of risk taking both in respect to profit theory and in relation to the theory of investment choice.[7] But hitherto there has been almost no empirical evidence on the actual behavior of in-

[6] See, for example, *Share Ownership in the United States*, by Lewis H. Kimmel (Brookings Institution, Washington, 1952), and *Character and Extent of Over-the-Counter Markets*, by G. Wright Hoffman (University of Pennsylvania Press, 1952).

[7] See, for example, Irving Fisher's *Nature of Capital and Income* (New York, 1906); F. Lavington, *The English Capital Market* (London, 1921); J. M. Keynes, *A Treatise on Probability* (London, 1929) and *General Theory of Employment, Interest and Money* (London, 1936); G. L. S. Shackle, *Expectation in Economics* (Cambridge, 1949).

SUMMARY OF FINDINGS

dividuals toward risk taking. Upon examination of the corporate stock holdings of individuals by income group and by the size of corporate stock holdings themselves, it appears that the willingness to assume investment risks is greater at high than at low income levels, and that in any given income group the proportion of stockholdings that carry high investment risks is higher where the amount of stock held is small than where it is large. This finding bears out the conclusion reached by Friedman and Savage on theoretical grounds.[8]

From analysis of the characteristics of stock issues held by various income groups it is tentatively concluded that no rigid compartmentalization of equity markets exists but that there are gradual transitions in portfolio characteristics over the broad range of incomes. One suspects that some of the major observed differences in portfolio characteristics are reflections of the differing strength of various motives for investment for individuals in different economic strata of society.[9] But the evidence suggests that broad generalizations, advancing simple unitary theories of investment motivation for particular income groups, are not adequate to describe the actions of investors.

The foregoing are the principal findings of the present study and those that most directly relate to other investigations. A more detailed summary will be presented after a section acquainting the reader with the nature of the data from which the findings emerge.

Source of Data

The primary basis of the report is a sample of personal state income tax returns filed in Wisconsin in 1949 and showing income from financial assets of some type. Since individuals filing returns in that state are required to itemize the specific sources of all interest and dividend income, with the exception of interest from federal obligations, it was possible to make estimates of the dollar value of the interest- and dividend-bearing assets which they held. The sample itself was selected so as to insure that there were sufficient cases for analysis in all income groups; that is, upper income

[8] Milton Friedman and L. J. Savage, "The Utility Analysis of Choices Involving Risk," *Journal of Political Economy*, August 1948, pp. 279-304.

[9] There are very few studies of the motivations affecting investment behavior. An intensive analysis has been made by J. Keith Butters, Lawrence E. Thompson, and Lynn L. Bollinger in their *Effects of Taxation: Investment by Individuals* (Graduate School of Business Administration, Harvard University, 1953). Additional information has been obtained by the Survey of Consumer Finances and by Kimmel, *op. cit.*

SUMMARY OF FINDINGS

groups were oversampled proportionately to the lower income groups. When husband and wife filed separate returns, their incomes and estimated asset holdings were combined to obtain a picture for the unit as a whole. Returns of fiduciaries, partnerships, and corporations were excluded from the sample in order to confine the analysis to the investment practices of individuals. By relating the interest and dividend receipts of the individuals in the sample to an estimate of the distribution of interest and dividend receipts by income groups for all persons filing Wisconsin income tax returns in 1949, blow-up factors were obtained which when applied to the estimated value of holdings of the sampled individuals gave aggregate state estimates of holdings of the various assets surveyed.

Because most of the findings are based upon estimates derived from income tax returns, certain limitations must be accepted that are inherent in the returns. Not all persons with income file tax returns, and not all income received by persons filing returns is reported. While about three-fourths of all persons living in Wisconsin either file returns or are reported as dependents by those who do file returns, there undoubtedly exist a small but significant number of individuals who may be relatively important holders of financial assets but who do not file returns: pensioners with net taxable income less than the filing requirement ($800 for a single person or $1,600 for a married couple) are an example.

There is also considerable underreporting of income, particularly income from interest and dividends. It has been estimated on a country-wide basis that 60 per cent of all nonfederal cash-interest payments and 33 per cent of all corporate dividend payments in 1947 went unreported on federal income tax returns in that year. Not all of this, of course, represents tax evasion. Experience with the Wisconsin state income tax returns is roughly comparable. Whether the missing interest and dividend income is distributed proportionately to the distribution of such receipts which are reported, or whether underreporting is more prevalent in certain population strata than in others cannot be ascertained. Results of a sample audit of federal tax returns for 1948, however, suggest that underreporting of interest and dividend income is more prevalent in the lower than in the higher income groups and that the greater differential underreporting as between different income groups occurs in the case of income from interest. This would suggest that estimates of holdings understate the amounts held by the lower income groups to a greater extent than those held by the upper income groups, and

SUMMARY OF FINDINGS

that the understatement would be particularly great in the case of debt assets, i.e. those yielding interest receipts.

The types of financial assets covered by the survey include, of course, only those on which interest and dividend income must be reported on the tax returns. Three broad types are distinguishable: deposits and related claims (savings accounts in commercial and mutual savings banks, savings and loan association shares, credit union shares, and postal savings deposits); direct debt assets (corporate bonds, obligations of state, county and municipal authorities, and notes and mortgages); and finally, corporate stocks, both traded and untraded issues. The interest receipts from deposit types of assets and from notes and mortgages were capitalized at prevailing interest rates characteristic for the specific type of institution. Bond interest receipts were capitalized at specific interest rates for each issue discovered, and the resulting principal amount was adjusted to market value.[10] For traded stocks yearly dividend rates per share as indicated by the investment manuals were used to determine the number of shares of each issue held by persons in the sample, which when combined with price data allowed an estimate of the market value of the holdings. Dividends from untraded stocks were valued by reference to the Wisconsin corporate income tax returns to obtain an estimate of the book value of each holding of a particular issue. These book value estimates of untraded corporate stock holdings were then adjusted to a market value concept on the basis of known relationships between market and book value of stocks regularly traded.

The types of financial assets on which information is available from the Wisconsin tax returns account for about one-half of the total value of all financial assets held by individuals. The types of financial assets omitted from the Wisconsin survey because of lack of information include cash, demand deposits, insurance, and federal government obligations. Limited information on the ownership of demand deposits, savings bonds, and life insurance has been developed, however, from estimates of the Survey of Consumer Finances for the United States as a whole. Estimates for holdings of bonds in default and of stocks not paying dividends in 1949 are, of course, not available from income tax returns.

To the reader experienced in research it will be evident that there

[10] Par value was used instead of market value in the case of obligations of state, county, and municipal authorities because of inability to distinguish maturity of issues when, as was frequently the case, the obligor had several issues of varying maturity at the same interest rate.

SUMMARY OF FINDINGS

are important hidden qualifications to the data, in view of which the findings are stated with reserve. Consider, for illustration, the problems involved in selecting 1949 as the base year. During a substantial portion of the year industrial activity was at a cyclical low; the level of industrial workers' incomes therefore tended to be somewhat nonrepresentative, and their stockholdings (which appeared to be meager) were probably attributed in some cases to income groups in which they would not normally occur. If a two-year average of income had been used as the base, the effect of such cyclical changes might have been reduced and inequalities in the distribution of financial asset ownership (as well as income) might have appeared to be different. Again, some corporations failed to pay dividends in 1949 because of the depressed level of business, and ownership of their stocks would not appear in our data. For such reasons, and because of the inherent biases involved in using income tax data, no computation of sampling error has been made. Chance errors arising from sampling would appear to be relatively slight, and therefore scarcely worth measuring, as compared with errors potentially many times larger arising from other sources.

The Relation of Income to Asset Holdings

The 3,462 personal income tax returns in the sample (which in the case of married couples with both husband and wife reporting income had been put on a joint basis if not already so) showed incomes in 1949 ranging from a negative amount to slightly over $1 million. Negative income recipients, though mentioned in the tabulations, are excluded from the analysis because of the small number of cases; positive income recipients have been divided into five income groups, each with a sufficient number of cases for a somewhat detailed analysis. The classes used for most of the analysis are: $0 to $4,999, $5,000 to $9,999, $10,000 to $19,999, $20,000 to $49,999, and $50,000 and over.

As the financial asset holdings of different income classes are viewed in ascending order of income, a considerable shift in portfolio composition appears. Time deposits and related claims together with direct debt assets make up a heavy share of the holdings of individuals with less than $5,000 income; going up the scale, corporate stocks become progressively more important, until for the group with $50,000 income and over they make up 93.3 per cent of the total dollar value of the assets surveyed. There is also a shift within the debt category. For progressively higher income

SUMMARY OF FINDINGS

groups direct debt assets make up a greater proportion, and assets consisting of deposits and related claims a lesser proportion, of the ever smaller debt component of the holdings.

Differences in the composition of financial asset holdings as between income classes of the population are traceable to two underlying phenomena: variations in the frequency with which certain types of asset are held, and variations in the average size of holdings of particular types. In these respects our findings are in substantial agreement with the view that individuals tend to invest first in relatively safe though low yielding assets, and only after obtaining some minimum amount of safe reserves, together with or in lieu of a larger income, do they invest to any great extent in more speculative but higher yielding assets. Individuals in the highest income group ($50,000 and over) obtained almost twice as high a yield upon their total holdings of financial assets as did the lowest income group (under $5,000), and most of the difference appears to be attributable to the fact that the low income groups as a whole are heavily invested in low yielding time deposits and related claims while the highest income group is heavily invested in corporate stocks.

Not only does the relative importance of the major types of financial asset vary with the holder's income status. Within two of the three major asset types, also, shifts in the composition of holdings appear as successively higher income groups are considered. Within the category of direct debt assets there is a considerable shift from notes and mortgages of individuals, an important investment outlet in the lowest income group, to obligations of business concerns and tax-exempt bonds in the higher income groups. Of even greater interest is the variation in the composition of corporate stock holdings. In the lower income groups the holdings of corporate stock consist largely of traded issues of publicly owned corporations; for successively higher income groups, untraded issues of closely held corporations become increasingly important. Only in the case of time deposits and related claims is the composition apparently little affected by differences in holders' incomes.

The different composition of asset holdings at various levels of income and accompanying differences in the frequency with which various types of asset are held produce a considerable variation as between types of asset in the concentration of holdings as measured by dollar value. About three-quarters of the dollar value of time deposits and related claims is held by the lowest income group (under $5,000), and on the other hand about three-quarters of the

SUMMARY OF FINDINGS

dollar value of corporate stocks is held by income groups above the $5,000 level. Demand deposits, United States savings bonds, and life insurance all seem to be types of asset whose ownership tends to be concentrated predominantly in the lower income groups, at least in comparison with corporate equities. Although a correction for underreporting of interest and dividend receipts would probably increase the indicated holdings of both equity and deposit types of asset more for the lower than for the upper income groups, such a correction would probably tend to reinforce the conclusion that most savings bonds, deposits, and related claims are owned by the income groups under $10,000 and most corporate stock by the income groups over that figure.

The relation existing between the income level of the individual and the types of financial assets making up his investment portfolio appears to be complex and impossible of generalization. Certainly, both logical inference and the available facts point to the conclusion that in many cases it is the income level of the individual that tends to determine the broad outlines of portfolio composition. Upon evidence that affords only a crude measure of wealth (the amount of financial assets held), portfolio composition in the lower ranges of income seems to be somewhat more sharply affected by the income factor than by the wealth factor. On the other hand, income level itself for some individuals is more or less importantly determined by income from investments, and the type of investment held is of considerable importance in determining investment yields. In addition, undoubtedly some individuals are able to command superior executive salaries from closely held corporations because of control of the corporation through stock ownership. Finally, of course, certain individuals because of education and natural aptitudes might not only be able to command superior incomes but also be able to select the most productive investments. There are probably other factors tending to explain the complex lines of causation between portfolio composition and income, but they will not be gone into.

The Relation of Occupation and City Size to Type of Asset Holding

Along with income, occupation and city size are important factors affecting the pattern of ownership of financial assets. Individuals in the sample were classified by occupation as stated on the tax returns (in the case of a joint or combined return, as stated for the head of the unit), and by size of city according to residential mail-

SUMMARY OF FINDINGS

ing address and preliminary 1950 census population estimates. The analysis of the relation between these characteristics and financial asset holdings constitutes a major section of the study.

The most striking differences in frequency, concentration, and composition of asset holdings appear to be those connected with the occupational characteristics of the investor. Managerial and self-employed persons head or constitute about 10 per cent of the number of families and single persons in the United States. Among the sampled Wisconsin taxpayers, they made up 10 per cent of the holders of deposits and related claims, 18 per cent of the holders of direct debt assets, 20 per cent of the holders of traded stocks, and 28 per cent of the holders of untraded stocks. In value terms, however, the managerial and self-employed group was much more important, holding 14 per cent of the debt manifested by deposits and similar claims, 24 per cent of the direct debt, 31 per cent of the value of traded stocks, and 61 percent of the value of untraded stocks.

In value terms a second group is of almost equal importance—individuals not gainfully employed. Constituting about 20 per cent of the population (that is, of the number of families and single persons), the group includes unemployed and retired persons, and those living on property incomes, insurance proceeds, gifts, etc.[11] In the Wisconsin survey material it includes, besides, some individuals whose occupation could not be determined. Individuals "not gainfully employed" made up 12 per cent of the holders of deposits and related claims, 26 per cent of the holders of direct debt assets, 21 per cent of the holders of traded stocks, and 22 per cent of the number of holders of untraded stocks. In value terms the group not gainfully employed was much more important, holding 19 per cent of the deposits and related claims, 38 per cent of the direct debt, 42 per cent of the traded stocks, and 23 per cent of the value of untraded stocks. The holdings of the group, of course, are greatly weighted by a relatively small number of individuals whose occupation might be termed "investments"; that is, persons living almost exclusively on property income.

[11] A subgroup, "housewives," is shown separately; in the present sample it consists mainly of widows and single women living on income other than earnings. The income and assets of wives (whether or not gainfully employed) and of dependents (in the relatively few cases where a tax return reported income for them) were treated on a combined basis with those of the head of the unit. Cases where the returns showed that the husband worked only intermittently during 1949 and the unit was therefore classified under the wife's occupation were very few.

SUMMARY OF FINDINGS

The remaining occupational groups—about 70 per cent of the population—constituted one-half or more of the number of holders of each type of asset, but in terms of dollar value they were important only as holders of debt assets, owning 67 per cent of all deposits and related claims and 38 per cent of all direct debt assets. In contrast, they held only 27 per cent of the total value of traded stocks and a still smaller proportion of the value of untraded stocks (16 per cent).

Occupational differences are shown somewhat more clearly by examining the composition of the financial asset holdings of various occupational groups. For farmers, semiskilled and skilled workers, and unskilled workers, time deposits and similar claims were important as compared with other assets. In the holdings of farmers, unskilled workers, and retired persons direct debt assets were also important. Groups having the largest concentration of traded stocks include professional persons, housewives, and individuals not gainfully employed. Only the group of managerial and self-employed individuals had a relatively high concentration of untraded stocks. In some of the occupational groups, typical income differences are important in explaining asset composition; thus only for farmers in the higher income ranges, rather than for all farmers, were debt assets an important part of holdings. In other groups income level was less important; for example, housewives in all income ranges held a large proportion of their assets in the form of traded stocks.

Differences in the composition of the financial asset holdings of individuals according to the size of community in which they live appear to be largely associated with the typical form of business organization found in communities of different sizes. Thus, in rural areas and small towns, where firms commonly are unincorporated proprietorships or partnerships, time deposits and related claims and direct debt instruments seem more important than in cities. In medium-sized cities characterized by small corporations, untraded stock issues are more important than in rural areas. In metropolitan centers, such as Milwaukee, traded corporate stocks—as a rule, issues of large corporations—have great importance. Income differentials between communities of various sizes are not sufficient to explain these tendencies, since in general they are apparent even within income stratifications.

The findings on the relationship of financial asset holdings to occupation and city size suggest that two important factors in the allocation of personal investment are the ability to invest in a business in which the investor is affiliated and the preference for local

SUMMARY OF FINDINGS

investment. The importance of these factors was tested directly in the case of corporate stocks.

In order to determine the importance of stock ownership by persons who are employees or officers of the corporation whose stock they hold, notation was made of all stocks in corporations from which the owner was receiving wages, salaries, or directors' fees. The blown-up estimates of the dollar value of holdings of such "business interest" stocks represented little more than 10 per cent of the holdings of traded issues but about two-thirds of the total value of untraded or closely held issues. Moreover, in the case both of traded and of untraded issues, business interest holdings increased in importance with the income level of the investor.

The preference for stock ownership in local concerns was tested in the case of traded issues only, since a large proportion of untraded issues were business interest holdings and therefore might be expected to be issues of local corporations. About 30 per cent of the value of traded issues held by Wisconsin individuals was found to consist of issues of corporations carrying out major production operations within the state. Furthermore, the result did not change when the tabulation was confined to holdings which were not of the business interest type.

These findings appear to shed new light on some of the problems faced in raising new equity capital for business enterprise. Apparently new and small companies may expect that one of the "costs" of capital will be a voice in the active management of the business, and that equity capital will be forthcoming in significant amounts only from certain occupational groups and from persons living in the immediate geographic area. Whether institutional arrangements may be set up to circumvent these difficulties is, of course, beyond the scope of this inquiry.

Characteristics of Traded Stock Holdings

In the process of estimating the value of traded stock held by all individuals in the universe sampled, it was necessary to assemble information on the 1949 price of the stock issues involved and the dividends paid per share. Accordingly, with a little additional effort it was possible to assemble information about other characteristics of stock issues held by sampled individuals—information such as the market in which the issues are traded, industry classification, yield, type of stock (i.e. common or preferred), and agency rating grade. An important part of the study was the attempt to relate the

SUMMARY OF FINDINGS

characteristics of traded stock issues to the income levels of the holders. The aim was twofold: first, to learn more about the motives for corporate equity ownership and the relation of income level to such motivation; second, to determine whether the individual market for corporate equities is a compartmentalized market, with different income groups holding separate types of stock, or whether the individual market for corporate equities is approximately homogeneous, with all income groups having about equal preference for all types of stocks. Two supplementary investigations were also included: the relation of turnover and of diversification to income of holder.

It is difficult to give an unequivocal statement of what is meant by differences in the market characteristics of stocks. In general, stocks traded on the New York Stock Exchange are those of large corporations with wide public ownership and some speculative appeal. Stocks traded on the American Stock Exchange are quite similar, although they tend to be issues of somewhat smaller corporations. Stocks traded on regional exchanges are quite likely to be less widely distributed, and those traded over the counter—with some exceptions, such as investment trust stocks—still less widely distributed. Perhaps the clearest general difference between types of market is that shown by the relative degree of turnover: stocks traded on the New York Stock Exchange have about twice the degree of turnover of stocks traded on regional exchanges and over the counter, while stocks traded on the American Stock Exchange experience about 50 per cent higher turnover than those traded on regional exchanges and over the counter. The degree of turnover is, of course, a crude measure of the degree of liquidity afforded to the issues traded in particular markets. Within each type of market, however, particular issues differ greatly in turnover, and over-all measures of turnover have all the faults usually inherent in such general measures.

When holdings of traded stocks for various income groups (including stocks regularly traded over the counter on which 1949 price and dividend information could be obtained) are viewed in ascending order of income, a slight shift is observed, in terms of dollar value, from issues traded on the New York Stock Exchange and the American Stock Exchange to issues traded on regional exchanges and over the counter. If untraded stock is included as part of the issues traded over the counter, the shift becomes considerably greater because of the proportionately heavier holdings of untraded stocks in the higher versus the lower income groups. Part

SUMMARY OF FINDINGS

of this difference in the market characteristics of stocks owned by various income groups may be the effect of real differences in preference for easily liquidated investment. Not all of it, however; for in part it reflects the uneven distribution of business interest holdings, which are more prevalent in the upper than in the lower income ranges, and many of which undoubtedly comprise issues that are traded on regional exchanges and over the counter.

The traded stock holdings of various income groups differ quite sharply according to the nature of the industry of the issuing corporation. In the lower income groups the stocks of investment trusts, utility companies operating in Wisconsin, and the American Telephone and Telegraph Company are important, as are issues of oil and gas extraction and integrated petroleum companies. In the higher income groups, stocks of pulp and paper, iron and steel, nonelectrical machinery, and trade corporations are important. In general the stock of manufacturing corporations is of considerably greater importance in the higher than in the lower income groups.

With some exceptions, these findings on the industry classification of stocks held by various income groups are roughly what might be expected if the lower income groups generally followed a conservative investment policy while the upper income groups followed a more speculative policy—at least if the traditional division of industries into conservative and speculative categories is accepted. Such a view, of course, does not explain the greater importance of petroleum stocks in the holdings of the lowest income group than for others, nor does it explain why many of the stockholders in the higher income groups—and among them, some investors holding twenty or more issues—were holders of stock in investment trusts.

Another instance consistent with the view that the lower income groups generally follow a conservative investment policy, while the upper income groups hold more speculative positions, is found in the analysis of the division between preferred and common shares in the traded stock holdings of various income groups. There is considerable variation in that respect along the income scale. About 15 per cent of the dollar value of traded stocks held by the lowest income group (under $5,000) consists of preferred issues, while only about 6 per cent of the amount held by the highest income group ($50,000 and over) represents preferred issues. In the case of untraded issues, the greater importance of preferred stocks in the holdings of the lower income groups is even more marked. These findings may be indicative of differences between income

SUMMARY OF FINDINGS

groups in attitudes toward risk taking, but undoubtedly much of the ownership of common issues in the higher income groups may be adjudged to be motivated by the desire for a voice in the control of corporate policy, particularly when the reason for a relatively high income may be attributed to the ownership of business interest stocks.

A more direct test of the relation between the income level of the investor and the quality of stocks held than is afforded by an analysis of industry characteristics or an analysis of the division between common and preferred issues was attempted by an examination of the agency rating grades of the traded stocks held.[12] Only those issues bearing ratings were included in the analysis; therefore issues of investment trusts, banks, insurance companies, and holding companies were excluded. In all, issues accounting for about three-quarters of the value of traded stocks held by Wisconsin individuals were included in the analysis.

As the portfolios of rated stocks of progressively higher income groups were considered, it was found that even though smaller proportions of the aggregate dollar value of holdings consisted of prime risk issues, there was only a slight shift into the most speculative issues. Considering the proportions of stock of all the various grades, the average risk for the aggregate portfolio of the highest income group ($50,000 and over) was about two-fifths of one grade higher than the average risk for the lowest group (with incomes of less than $5,000).

If, instead of measuring differences in risk taking in value terms, the risk-taking propensities of individuals in various income groups are measured without regard to differences in the amount of stock held, a slightly different picture is obtained. The lowest income group shows the greatest diversity of practices, having the largest proportions of individuals with either extremely safe or extremely risky positions in regard to their rated stocks, while the middle and upper income groups have the greatest proportions of stockholders with moderate risk positions.

Part of the reason why the difference in the propensity to assume investment risk, as shown by holdings of rated stock, was not greater than two-fifths of one rating grade between the lowest and highest income groups appears to lie in the inverse relationship between the quality and the amount of traded stocks held. Individuals

[12] The agency ratings used are those published by the Fitch Publishing Company for December 1949.

were divided into groups according to the amount of traded stock holdings as well as by income, in order to determine the separate effects of each variable. In general, if individuals with the same amount of traded stock holdings but different income are considered, those in the higher income groups have positions of greater risk than those with lower incomes. On the other hand, if individuals in the same income class—but with different amounts of traded stock holdings—are considered, those with large amounts of traded stock holdings have more conservative positions, in general, than those with small amounts. Since there are many stockholders in the low income groups with small amounts of stocks, the apparent tendency for many of them to hold relatively speculative positions probably offsets, at least in some degree, the conservative positions of other individuals in the same income range.

The findings on differences in risk taking as between different income groups suggest that any simple generalization about the relation of income to risk is dangerous. There is a positive association between income and risk taking; yet individuals holding relatively risky positions make up a larger proportion of all stockholders in the lower than in the higher income groups. In part this seems to be accounted for by the fact that risk taking is negatively associated with the amount of the investment, and the low income groups include large numbers of individuals with only small holdings of traded stocks. There may well be, also, considerable geographic and temporal difference in the outlook of various income groups on the assumption of risk.

Do the higher income groups obtain higher yields (1949 dividends related to value) on their stockholdings than the lower income groups? So far as untraded stock holdings are concerned the answer is definitely yes, if book value rather than market price is taken as the basis of valuation. There is a difference of approximately two percentage points between the yield on the untraded stocks held by the lowest income group (under $5,000) and the yield on those held by the highest income group ($50,000 and over), and there is a fairly constant upward progression for successively higher income groups. On the other hand, the picture is less clear in the case of traded issues. For the first four income groups in ascending order, the yield on traded issues falls perceptibly, and then for the highest income group ($50,000 and over) it rises.

Some part of the irregular behavior of traded stock yields along

SUMMARY OF FINDINGS

the income scale may result from the fact that in 1949 medium grade stocks had a higher yield than did either the prime quality or the most speculative issues. The topmost income group, since it had the greatest proportion of its total portfolio of traded stocks in the medium grade category, might well be expected to obtain higher yields than the lower income groups, where holdings were characterized by greater diversity in quality. Probably no simple explanation is sufficient to account for differences between income groups in yields obtained on stockholdings. It has been suggested, for instance, that individuals with high incomes could benefit from the standpoint of tax liability by purchasing issues of corporations which retained most of their earnings; that is, by choosing capital gains realized over a period of years rather than current dividends. If such a practice were followed, one would expect lower current yields in the higher than in the lower income groups. This expectation is clearly not borne out in the case of untraded stock; and for traded securities, yields fall slightly for successively higher income groups up to the $50,000 level, then turn up sharply.[13]

As might be expected, diversification in traded stock holdings increases both with the income of the individual and with the amount of stocks held. In the lowest income group (under $5,000) about two-fifths of the individuals holding traded stock were found to hold only one issue, and the average number of issues held was not quite four. In the highest income group ($50,000 and over) only about one-eighth of the individuals had but one issue, and the average number of issues held was eighteen. Similar differences in degree of diversification are found when individuals are ranked according to the size of their traded stock holdings. For those holding less than $500 the average number of issues held was not much above one; for those holding traded stocks valued at $1 million or more the average was thirty-five different issues.

What income groups experience the greatest turnover of their traded stock holdings relative to the total value of the holdings? For all income groups the average value of stocks sold in 1949 was approximately 7 per cent of total holdings. Generally, the highest income group ($50,000 and over) experienced the lowest

[13] I am indebted to Daniel M. Holland of the National Bureau of Economic Research for pointing out that my test is indicative of the results spelled out above, but not conclusive. My test indicates that for income groups in ascending order the ratio of dividends to book value for untraded stocks increases. This does not, however, demonstrate that the ratio of dividends to earnings also increases, which is the relevant consideration.

rate of turnover (about 4 per cent) while the income groups with $5,000 to $20,000 experienced the highest (about 8 per cent). It might be expected from the turnover figures that individuals in the low and medium income groups hold their shares for a shorter period of time than do those in the higher income groups, and tabulations of stocks sold during 1949 according to date of purchase appear to confirm that belief.

Price per share for traded stock issues held by various income groups was the last of the characteristics analyzed. Price behavior over the cycle has been observed to be somewhat more variable for issues with a low price per share than for issues with a relatively high price per share. This has sometimes led to the belief that low priced shares are favored by the lower income groups, whose purchases and sales are thought to vary greatly over the cycle. There is some evidence to indicate that proportionately more of the individuals in the lower and middle income groups had stockholdings with a low average price ($20 per share and under) than in the higher income groups; but there is also evidence that the proportion of individuals with relatively high priced stock holdings ($50 per share and over) was greater in the lower than in the higher income groups. The reason for this apparently contradictory evidence appears to lie in a combination of factors: in the positive association between quality and price per share, and in the fact that lower income individuals, as was observed earlier, tend toward greater extremes in risk position than do higher income individuals. If the analysis is confined to issues of the same quality, a positive association between income and price per share is found only in the case of low quality stocks, the reverse apparently being the case with high quality stocks.

Suggested Areas for Further Research

Perhaps the greatest need for research in the area with which we are concerned here is to determine whether, in fact, the flow of savings into investment through time is similar to that inferred by an examination of holdings of financial assets at one point in time. It has been remarked that changes in the economic status of individuals, inheritance, and change in the valuations of the assets themselves all act to distort the picture of the flow of savings that is obtained from an examination of holdings. It is likely that other factors also act to change the flow of funds from saving arising in particular income groups and going into particular channels. One of the most interesting speculations is whether there are cyclical movements in investment preferences or whether individuals' patterns of preference as to saving and investment are fairly constant, varying largely in response to changes in income.

Perhaps almost equally important to an understanding of the flow of funds is the task of determining the reasons for major changes in the ownership of already existing financial assets. This topic also needs investigation from a cyclical standpoint. At times the theory has been proposed that a stock market boom is characterized by an enlarged distribution of stock ownership among the lower income groups, accompanied by a withdrawal of the higher income groups from corporate equity ownership, and that the reverse happens in declining markets. It is highly important that changes in the ownership of financial assets be explored at length to determine whether they accompany broad changes in the prices of such assets.

There are, of course, many ways of making a study with a time dimension. One obvious way is to draw comparable samples separated in time and to adjust the differences for known changes, such as changes in prices. This is not impossible to do from tax data, although the magnitude of the operation increases with the number of years to be covered. Another obvious method would be to interview investors; but the difficulty of obtaining data for past years by that means becomes greater the farther back one attempts to go, and the sampling problem seems to be more difficult in the interview approach, particularly with those income and occupational groups which contribute most of the savings and a major portion of equity funds.

One very important area of investigation is the psychological attitudes toward such factors as risk and liquidity. The few studies that have been made seem to have penetrated only a short distance into the motives for preferences in regard to risk and liquidity and why preferences appear to differ at different income levels. Because these matters lie at the bottom of much thinking in the fields of investment, interest theory, and taxation, it is surprising that so little work has been done upon them.

Finally, one cannot help but be struck with the paucity of data on the characteristics of corporate stocks. Historical records exist showing price, yield, earnings, some estimate of grade, and the like over many years; but investigation into the market behavior of stocks has largely been pointed toward discovering profit possibilities in particular securities rather than toward forming general conclusions about particular types and classes of stock. It would be interesting, for example, to determine whether the backward-turning yield curve shown on page 129 is true generally or only in certain years. These are studies that immediately come to mind; undoubtedly many other facets of inquiry that are touched on in the body of this report would prove fruitful areas for research.

CHAPTER 2

Financial Asset Ownership and the Flow of Savings and Investment

PART of the wealth owned by individuals consists of financial assets—bonds, stocks, bank accounts, and the like—which are not items of material wealth in themselves but only claims against tangible wealth. In some respects, however, their significance is equivalent to that of the material wealth they represent, and the processes by which they are created and extinguished are among those most crucial to the proper functioning of the economy. When an individual purchases a financial asset, he is in effect allowing some other individual or company to use his funds. Although the purchase does not necessarily mean that individual savings are being channeled into real investment, net increments to the stock of financial assets owned by all individuals which are not offset by increases in the cash balances of the issuers (or by decreases in their indebtedness to the banking system) result in a flow of savings into real investment, provided the increments do not arise solely from price increases.

Recent economic thinking emphasizes the tenuous nature of the connection between saving and investment processes, recognizing that in a highly industrialized economy a considerable part of all real investment is performed by persons and organizations other than those doing the saving. Financial assets provide a link, so to speak, in the indirect connection between saving and investment. From that standpoint our interest in the distribution of ownership of financial assets stems from the fact that analysis of it may cast some light on the sources of saving and the manner in which individuals choose to allocate their savings among different outlets.

More specifically, we are interested in determining how different types of financial assets are distributed among individuals classified according to their income, their occupation, and the size of the city in which they reside, stratifications of society which are regarded as important in accounting not only for the economic behavior of individuals but also for their actions in other respects. Apart from the purely descriptive aspect of the problem, we are interested in discovering functional relationships between the characteristics of the individual and his actions as a financial investor. It is of interest to ascertain whether such functional relationships exist, even though we may lack the means to obtain precise quantitative measurements of them. A knowledge of functional relationships in this area is important in many respects, and it is hoped that the present study will make some contribution to it.

The means by which one may study how individuals with different economic and social characteristics allocate their current savings among different outlets are distinctly limited, particularly if emphasis is to be placed on their purchases of corporate stocks. Individuals may be selected at random from the population and interviewed to find out how much they saved and what they did with their savings. Interview surveys from a broad population base, however, encounter serious difficulties when used as the basis for estimating dollar value of asset holdings, because of the reluctance of many individuals to discuss their financial position. Since interview surveys usually encounter poor response in the upper income groups—the very groups whose holdings of financial assets bulk largest—quantitative estimates of aggregate holdings are frequently seriously underestimated. Furthermore, unless the sample is extremely large, there are seldom enough cases for detailed analysis of the characteristics of the owners of types of financial assets which are not widely distributed among the population. In spite of these defects, interview surveys can make a real contribution to the explanation of the investment behavior of individuals, particularly in probing the motivation behind investor action.[1]

If dollar value estimates of holdings of the less widely distributed types of financial assets are desired, together with considerable detailed information about both the holder and the specific securities held, one is virtually forced to rely upon information compiled from record data obtained for other purposes. Such record data may consist of customer records of brokerage firms, stock ownership records of corporations themselves, or estate and income tax returns.

In effect, this last source is the one used for the present study. Estimates of the financial asset holdings of individuals have been obtained from an analysis of 3,462 Wisconsin state income tax returns for the year 1949 (single returns, or joint or combined

[1] See the work of Butters, Thompson, and Bollinger cited in Chapter 1 (footnote 9) for an example of a study designed to overcome the usual difficulties of interview surveys.

returns of husband and wife where both reported income). The fact that specific sources of each item of interest and dividend income must be reported by the individual taxpayer in that state makes it possible to estimate, along lines described in Chapter 3, the value of certain types of financial asset holdings. The particular merit of this approach is that one can obtain a rather detailed estimate of corporate stock holdings, and thus cast light upon some of the problems of equity finance. An allied advantage is that the upper income groups are well covered by tax reports, so that their role in business finance can be given due attention.

There are disadvantages to the approach, however. In the first place, the data constitute only a cross section of financial asset holdings at one point in time, and do not reveal how current savings are allocated to investment over a period of time. In the second place, cross-section studies of individual behavior do not show, except by implication, how an individual's actions are affected by a change in his status. It is thought, for example, that if an individual's income increases he will not immediately assume the behavior characteristic of the new income level as regards saving, but will instead be influenced by the recency of the change in his income and by his past income level. Financial investment behavior probably responds similarly. Nevertheless, cross-section studies do show the direction which changes are likely to take.

A further complication inherent in studies of the present type is that they attempt to show how individuals invest their current savings by an analysis of the composition of assets accumulated over a period of years. Yet it is clear that (1) individuals may invest new savings out of income in quite different forms and proportions than are indicated by the forms in which they hold accumulated assets, (2) the amount originally invested is not shown when assets are valued at current prices, and (3) the status of the individual when some of the currently held assets were acquired may have been different from his present economic and social position. Nothwithstanding these defects, a knowledge of the distribution of financial assets in relation to the current social and economic position of the holder is a useful first step in clarifying some of the relationships between the saving and investment processes.

In this chapter the object is to give perspective to the analysis of the asset holdings of Wisconsin individuals by drawing on supplementary sources for over-all information on the characteristics of the individuals who provide the bulk of all savings, on the manner in which individuals allocate their savings among different investment outlets, and on the relationship of their current purchases of financial assets to their total stock. The purpose is not only to add quantitative perspective to the material which is to follow, but also to set forth explicitly some of the conceptual problems which arise when one attempts to infer the sources of savings, and its allocation, from the distribution of financial asset holdings.

The Sources of Saving

Net new saving can be contributed to by individuals acting solely on personal account, by business firms, or by governmental units. While it is fairly easy to segregate savings originating or being absorbed in the governmental sphere, it is less easy to distinguish between individual and business saving. In national income accounting the corporate sphere is treated separately, mainly because estimates of corporate saving are derived from different sources than are estimates of personal saving. Most of the saving attributed to corporations undoubtedly originates in that sphere,[2] whereas a considerable amount of personal saving may in fact be business saving done by the owners of unincorporated firms and left in the business. In all but the worst periods of depression, when the owners of unincorporated businesses tend to draw money out of their firms for personal use, between 10 and 25 per cent of the saving attributed to the personal sector probably has been saving by unincorporated business firms.[3]

In 1949, gross private saving amounted to $37 billion, of which some $21 billion represented inventory valuation adjustments, capital outlays charged to current expense, depreciation allowances of corporations, etc., and $9 billion was undistributed corporate profits.[4] The remaining $7 billion probably consisted of $5.3 billion of saving solely by individuals and about $1.7 billion left in unincorporated business firms.[5] If new saving is defined as the

[2] The saving done by personal holding companies should probably not be considered business saving, even though it is done through a corporate form of organization.

[3] Simon Kuznets, *National Income and Its Composition, 1919-1938* (National Bureau of Economic Research, 1941), Vol. I, Table 39, p. 276.

[4] *Survey of Current Business* (Department of Commerce), July 1952, Table 5, p. 16.

[5] Estimated by applying the approximate relationship between the saving of entrepreneurs and of other individuals prevailing in the relatively prosperous period 1919-28, as shown by Kuznets, to total personal saving in 1949, as estimated by the Department of Commerce.

saving of individuals plus net unincorporated business saving, plus corporate undistributed profits, then individual saving in 1949 represented about one-third of the total.[6] The saving of individuals, although low in 1949 as compared with other sources of saving, has historically been the most important source.[7]

What are the sources of individual saving? Fortunately there is fairly good evidence on the relative importance of the different groups contributing to total personal saving in 1949 in the Survey of Consumer Finances conducted by the Survey Research Center of the University of Michigan for the Board of Governors of the Federal Reserve System.[8] These data are roughly similar to those compiled by the Department of Commerce in that they include an unknown proportion of saving accumulated by unincorporated business, but they differ in excluding the saving of personal trust funds and nonprofit institutions.[9] Some of the findings on the sources of individual saving are shown in Table 1.

The Survey of Consumer Finances found that in 1949 the one-fifth of the spending units[10] that ranked highest in income accounted for 45 per cent of the total income received by individuals (Table 1). While that group received nearly half of all income, it contributed a great deal more than half of all net saving. Indeed, it provided 131 per cent of total net saving—enough to allow the lower income groups to spend more than they earned, through borrowing and disinvestment of liquid assets. The performance of the top quintile is all the more remarkable since about one-fourth of its units had zero or negative saving. Thus only about 15 per cent of the total population contributed positively to the high amount of saving shown for the highest income quintile.

[6] There is reason to believe that prevailing accounting practices result in an overstatement of corporate net saving in the years following World War II, and thus that the contribution of individual saving to total new net saving was probably understated in 1949.

[7] Kuznets, *op. cit.*, p. 276.

[8] "1950 Survey of Consumer Finances," *Federal Reserve Bulletin*, November 1950, pp. 1441-55.

[9] See *ibid.*, Appendix I, pp. 1452-53 for other differences.

[10] The Survey of Consumer Finances uses the concept of a "spending unit" rather than the family or single person. The spending unit consists of related persons living in the same household who pool their income for major expenses, or of a person who lives with relatives but whose finances are separate from theirs. Hence a family may contain one or more spending units. The Survey also includes persons living singly in private residences, but excludes residents of hotels and large boarding houses as well as the institutional population. Thus there are substantial differences between the Survey of Consumer Finances and the survey of Wisconsin taxpayers in the definition of the universe and the sampling unit.

TABLE 1
Comparative Saving by Income and Occupational Groups of Spending Units in the United States, 1949

CHARACTERISTIC OF SPENDING UNIT	PROPORTION OF POPULATION OF SPECIFIED GROUP	PROPORTION OF TOTAL ACCOUNTED FOR BY THE GROUP — Net Saving[a]	PROPORTION OF TOTAL ACCOUNTED FOR BY THE GROUP — Income[b]	PROPORTION OF UNITS PERFORMING POSITIVE SAVING
Income Rank, 1949				
Highest tenth	10%	105%	30%	} 78%
Second	10	26	15	
Third	10	13	12	} 70
Fourth	10	8	11	
Fifth	10	1	9	} 64
Sixth	10	c	8	
Seventh	10	−4	6	} 50
Eighth	10	−8	5	
Ninth	10	−6	3	} 37
Lowest tenth	10	−35	1	
Occupation				
Professional and semi-professional	7%	12%	11%	69%
Managerial and self-employed	12	54	21	71
Clerical and sales	13	14	13	65
Skilled and semiskilled	27	21	28	64
Unskilled and service	12	3	9	55
Farm operator	9	7	7	55
All other[d]	20	−11	11	50
All Spending Units	100%	100%	100%	60%

Data are from "1950 Survey of Consumer Finances," *Federal Reserve Bulletin*, November 1950, Tables 2, 3, 4, and 16, pp. 1442-43 and 1448, except the income distribution by occupation, which was computed from means shown in the *Federal Reserve Bulletin*, August 1950, Table 2, p. 950.

[a] Represents positive saving (money income in excess of expenditures) less negative savings (expenditures in excess of money income).

[b] Represents annual money income before taxes.

[c] Less than 0.5%.

[d] Includes farm laborers, students, housewives, protective workers, retired and unemployed persons, and those for whom occupation was not ascertained.

What about the distribution of saving among various occupational groups? In 1949, spending units in the managerial and self-employed group—constituting only 12 per cent of the total number of units—received approximately 21 per cent of the income and accounted for over half of the total net saving (Table 1). Although to some extent a high saving level would be expected because of the high average income level of that occupational group, the evidence suggests that managerial and self-employed individuals save more than other groups irrespective of income. Professional and semiprofessional persons, whose incomes in 1949 averaged only slightly less than those of managerial and self-employed persons ($5,350 as against $5,630), may be used as a standard of comparison. While the professional group saved 5.6 per cent of their income, the managerial group saved 14 per cent of theirs.[11]

Conceivably such a result could occur if one of the distributions contained a few individuals with extremely high incomes while the other did not, but the apparent differences between the two income distributions for the different occupations are too slight to suggest an influence of that kind. Furthermore, the proportion of persons saving large amounts of their income was considerably greater for the managerial than for the professional group. One-third of the units in the managerial and self-employed group had savings of $1,000 or more in 1949, while less than one-fourth of the professional group had savings of that amount.[12] It would appear, therefore, that although high average income may partially explain the large proportion of net saving accounted for by managerial and self-employed individuals, income level is not the full explanation of their high saving propensities.

The Flow of Personal Savings into Investment

The flow of savings from their origin in the personal sector of the economy to their specific use cannot be traced in optimum detail because of both conceptual and technical difficulties. The saving of individuals (as has been pointed out) cannot be segregated from the saving of unincorporated business firms. The conventional method of measuring investment used in national income accounting does not distinguish net new investment expenditures from expenditures intended only to maintain existing capital; nor is it possible to segregate investment expenditures paid for out of saving from those paid for out of borrowed funds. Thus although the totality of funds available from the personal sector for investment equals the totality of uses of those funds, to isolate the sources and uses of the saving of individual, exclusive of borrowed funds and exclusive of expenditures by unincorporated businesses for maintaining existing capital and for increasing capi-

---

[11] "1950 Survey of Consumer Finances," *Federal Reserve Bulletin*, August 1950, Table 2, p. 950.
[12] "1950 Survey of Consumer Finances," *Federal Reserve Bulletin*, November 1950, Appendix Table 1, p. 1454.

tal, is impossible. Even so, available data do reveal some interesting facets of the flow of personal saving into investment.

Table 2 uses Department of Commerce and Securities and Exchange Commission data to reconstruct the saving and investment activities of the personal sector of the economy in 1949. Included in the figures are saving and investment by unincorporated business firms, trust funds, and nonprofit institutions as well as saving and investment by individuals, with which we are most directly concerned. Net new saving from those sources, plus the depreciation allowances of unincorporated business firms and the net borrowing by individuals from banks and financial intermediaries, constitute, in our definition, the total of investment funds that became available within the year from the personal sector.[13]

The funds newly available from the personal sector for investment in 1949—amounting to nearly $27 billion—were invested in two ways: about two-thirds of the total was invested directly by the units accumulating the funds, either through purchases of residential housing or through investment in unincorporated business firms and farms; the remaining one-third was channeled into financial assets. The acquisition of such assets represented the contribution of investment funds by individuals and noncorporate business to other sectors of the economy. When financial assets increased by some $9 billion in 1949, both an increase in the claims of the personal sector against other sectors of the economy and a flow of investment funds resulted. The acquisition of financial assets thus originated as part of the process whereby personal saving flows into investment; but the data in Table 2 do not show what part of the net change in any given type of financial asset represented a use of funds arising from individual saving (rather than from individual borrowing or from the various activities of noncorporate business that were also sources of funds).

Other details on the disposition of funds from personal saving in 1949 are provided by the Survey of Consumer Finances, in data showing the percentage of spending units that reported additions to and withdrawals from various types of assets and liabilities (Table 3). Although the concepts of saving and the basic unit of analysis differ from those used by the Department of Commerce and the Securities and Exchange Commission, the results in them-

[13] This method of accounting shows only intersector flows and neglects the changes taking place within the personal sector. Transactions in which individuals borrow from each other or individuals invest in noncorporate business are ignored.

TABLE 2
Sources and Uses of Net New Investment Funds of the Personal Sector, 1949

Sources and Uses	Amount (billions)
SOURCES OF INVESTMENT FUNDS	
Net saving[a]	$8.99
Depreciation allowances	9.19
Net increases in debt to banks, intermediaries, and corporations	8.73
Total Funds for Investment	$26.91
USES OF INVESTMENT FUNDS	
Direct Investment	*$16.89*
Net purchases of nonfarm houses	7.04
New construction and producers' durable equipment expenditures[b]	10.83
Inventory changes[c]	−0.98
Investment in Financial Assets (net change)	9.16
Currency and bank deposits	−1.27
Savings and loan association shares	1.48
U.S. government securities	1.24
State and local government bonds	0.60
Private insurance and pension reserves	3.71
Government insurance and pension reserves	2.34
Corporate and other securities	1.06
Statistical Discrepancy	0.85
Total Personal Investment	$26.91

From *Survey of Current Business* (Department of Commerce), July 1952, Table 6, p. 16. Amounts will not always add to total because of rounding.

[a] Includes saving of individuals, unincorporated business firms, and farmers, plus the increase in government insurance and pension reserves.

[b] Includes expenditures by unincorporated business firms, farmers, and non-profit institutions.

[c] Includes inventory changes of unincorporated business firms and farmers.

selves and in connection with Table 2 indicate some important characteristics of the process whereby individual savings are channeled into investment.

First, it is shown that the proportion of units adding to their holdings differs substantially for different types of asset. Nearly three-quarters of the spending units added to their holdings of life insurance, while only 3 per cent added to their personal investments in unincorporated businesses and only 2 per cent increased their holdings of securities other than federal government bonds. Second, the data reveal wide differences in the ratio of units increasing to units diminishing their holdings of particular types of asset. Most

TABLE 3
Proportion of Spending Units in the United States Reporting Various Types of Additions to or Withdrawals from Savings, 1949

Form of Saving or Dissaving	Proportion of Units Reporting Change
Additions to Savings	
Increase in liquid asset holdings	26%
Payment of life insurance premium	74
Retirement fund payment	12
Increase in security holdings[a]	2
Profits left in unincorporated business[b]	2
Personal investment in unincorporated business[b]	3
Farm equipment purchase	4
Nonfarm home purchase	3
Other real estate purchase[c]	2
Payment on home mortgage[d]	17
Home improvement	14
Withdrawals from Savings	
Decrease in liquid asset holdings	31
Full cash payment from life insurance policy	3
Decrease in security holdings[a]	1
Losses from unincorporated business[b]	1
Withdrawal of investment in unincorporated business[b]	1
Mortgage for home purchase	2
Mortgage on other real estate	1
Sale of houses, farms, and lots	3

From "1950 Survey of Consumer Finances," *Federal Reserve Bulletin*, November 1950, Table 5, p. 1443.
[a] Excludes holdings of federal securities.
[b] Excludes farms.
[c] Includes farms.
[d] Includes full payments.

units reporting changes in their life insurance holdings reported increases, but approximately as many units reported decreases in their security holdings as reported increases, and slightly more units reported decreases in their liquid assets than reported increases. This analysis of the behavior of spending units, when it is contrasted with net changes in the dollar value of various types of asset holdings as shown in Table 2, suggests real differences in the types of individuals utilizing the various asset forms as outlets for their savings.

The crucial question involves the characteristics of the individuals who acquired the different financial assets; but the aggregate figures on net purchases, as well as the percentages of units reporting increases and decreases in their holdings of particular types of asset, are of little help in that respect. The published tabulations of the Survey of Consumer Finances indicate that increases in holdings of aggregate liquid assets during 1949 were more prevalent in the upper than in the lower income groups, and, as might be expected, that the proportion of units reporting decreases was slightly greater in the lower and middle income groups than in the highest income group.[14] The distribution of current savings into various outlets other than liquid assets by income, occupational, and city size groups is not available from the published material.

The most recent available data giving detailed estimates of the allocation of current savings are those derived by the 1941 Survey of Spending and Saving in Wartime. These data for urban families and single persons are summarized in Table 4, which shows for each of nine income groups the percentage distribution of the net change in total assets among various types of asset. Because the changes in total assets may be caused by changes both in savings and in liabilities, the data, strictly speaking, do not show what happened to savings alone. In 1941, which probably was not a typical year, all income groups with the exception of the two lowest showed net increases in total assets. The picture is complicated, however, by the fact that except in the two highest income groups liquid assets other than federal securities were being disinvested in that year probably to a large extent for the purchase of federal government bonds.

Nevertheless, the pattern of distribution of current funds among investment outlets at various income levels appears fairly regular: U.S. government bonds and insurance (and presumably other liquid assets in a more normal year) were the predominant outlets for accumulated funds in the lower income groups, and investment in real estate (including owned homes) assumed greatest importance in the middle income groups; investments in nonfederal bonds and stocks and owned businesses became increasingly important in the higher income groups. No data have been published to show the detailed distribution of current funds for investment according to occupation of investor and size of city of residence.

There is a caveat to analyzing investment holdings in order to throw light on the saving process. When the flow of funds into investment results in an increase in the financial assets owned by

[14] "1950 Survey of Consumer Finances," *Federal Reserve Bulletin*, December 1950, Table 13, p. 1595.

ASSET OWNERSHIP AND FLOW OF SAVINGS

TABLE 4
Distribution of Average Net Change in Total Assets by Type of Asset, for Income Groups of Urban Spending Units in the United States, 1941

TYPE OF ASSET	Less than $500	$500-999	$1,000-1,499	$1,500-1,999	$2,000-2,499	$2,500-2,999	$3,000-4,999	$5,000-9,999	$10,000 & Over
Liquid assets[a]	−82%	−296%	−89%	−15%	−45%	−35%	−13%	19%	16%
U.S. government bonds[b]	...	95	29	28	15	9	8	9	10
Private and government insurance[c]	2	217	85	40	58	48	35	27	20
Real estate owned[d]	−12	−24	84	47	58	91	62	30	18
Loans made[e]	−7	−85	[f]	1	−2	[f]	[f]	[f]	−5
Other bonds and stocks	...	14	−5	1	[f]	−1	1	3	12
Investment in own business	−6	−23	18	1	17	−11	9	12	29
All other assets	5	2	−22	−3	−1	−1	−1	...	...
Total	−100%	−100%	100%	100%	100%	100%	100%	100%	100%
Average net change	$−104.74	$−8.09	$49.29	$170.37	$147.63	$235.67	$459.79	$1,258.70	$4,520.37

Compiled from data in *Family Spending and Saving in Wartime*, Bureau of Labor Statistics, Bulletin 822, April 1945, Table 35, pp. 187-88.
[a] Excludes U.S. government bonds; includes cash, savings accounts, checking accounts, and savings and loan association shares.
[b] Includes tax savings notes.
[c] Private insurance includes premium payments less surrendered and settled policies; government insurance includes social security and unemployment insurance tax payments.
[d] Includes owned home and other real estate purchases less sales plus improvements on such property holdings.
[e] Represents net change in the principal amount of loans made to others.
[f] Less than 0.5%.

36

individuals, these holdings are only partly, and not exclusively, the result of a saving process. The value of assets is seldom thought of as merely their original price, especially in times of rising general prices. Holdings thus represent a sum consisting of an original purchase price and a sum representing realized and unrealized capital gains (or losses), arising from changes in the market prices of assets involved.[15]

Turning now to the problem of adequacy of coverage: How much of the total financial assets held by individuals consists of types of assets covered by the survey of Wisconsin state income tax returns of individuals? Table 5 sets forth the estimated value of eleven types of assets held by the personal sector of the economy. The figures differ in concept from the estimates shown earlier, in Table 2, because holdings of trust funds and financial and non-profit institutions (as well as of corporations) have been excluded. Holdings of noncorporate business firms, including partnerships, are included. With allowances for the fact that asset holdings of partnerships have been omitted from the survey data to be presented in the following chapters but could not be excluded here, Table 5 should serve to indicate the relative importance of the types of asset included in the survey of Wisconsin investors.[16]

The items marked by an asterisk in Table 5 are those types of asset for which ownership estimates may be made from the Wisconsin individual income tax returns. For the United States as a whole these assets amount to $211.7 billion, or slightly over half of the $390.2 billion total for financial assets of all types held by individuals and noncorporate businesses in the United States. If we could exclude from Table 5 the financial assets held by noncorporate business and consider only holdings of individuals, it is likely that the percentage represented in the survey based upon tax returns would be even larger, since the excluded types of assets might be chiefly those which are impossible to trace through state tax returns—assets such as currency, demand deposits, insurance, and U.S. government securities.

[15] Since the market price of corporate stocks is affected at least theoretically by their book value, which frequently is, in turn, affected by additions to surplus from undivided profits, it is interesting to note that some changes in the market value of corporate stocks arise through corporate saving and thus are reflected in any analysis of personal saving which uses values of financial asset holdings as basic data.

[16] One further exception should be noted: the survey data do not include financial assets of noncorporate business held solely in the name of the business. Thus, securities held by noncorporate business firms would be included in Table 5 but excluded from the survey results shown in later chapters.

TABLE 5
Estimated Amount of Financial Assets Held by Individuals and Unincorporated Business Firms in the United States, 1949

Type of Financial Asset	Amount Held (billions)
1. Currency	$23.3
2. Demand deposits	39.2
3. Time deposits	55.8*
4. Savings and loan association shares	11.8*
5. U.S. government securities	47.0
6. Private insurance	60.0
7. Government insurance	9.0
8. Notes, mortgages, etc.	30.6*
9. State and local government bonds	6.0*
10. Corporate bonds[a]	7.0*
11. Corporate stocks[b]	100.5*
Total	$390.2

Asterisks mark types of asset for which estimates of individuals' holdings can be made from Wisconsin tax returns.

Items 1 through 5 are from "Estimated Liquid Asset Holdings of Individuals and Businesses," *Federal Reserve Bulletin*, July 1953, p. 720. Items 6 through 9 are unpublished staff estimates of the Board of Governors of the Federal Reserve System. Holdings of corporations, trust funds, and financial and nonprofit institutions are excluded. Other sources are noted below.

[a] Estimated from data of total outstandings in *The Volume of Corporate Bond Financing since 1900*, by W. Braddock Hickman (Princeton University Press for the National Bureau of Economic Research, 1953), Table A-1, p. 251. The original figure has been adjusted upward by $3.4 billion to include bonds of finance and real estate firms, and then reduced by $30.6 billion to exclude bonds held by financial intermediaries ($28.4 billion) and by trust funds ($2.2 billion).

[b] Estimated from Table A-2 of *The Share of Financial Intermediaries in National Wealth and National Assets, 1900-1949*, by Raymond W. Goldsmith (National Bureau of Economic Research, Occasional Paper 42, 1954). The original figure, which excludes intercorporate stock holdings, has been reduced to 23.6 per cent estimated to be held by financial intermediaries (*op. cit.*, p. 69).

Summary

In an attempt to give perspective to the detailed analysis of the investment practices of individuals which is to follow, data from supplementary sources have been presented in order to give the reader some basis for estimating the quantitative importance of the area under investigation as well as some acquaintance with the problems and concepts involved in such a study. It has been shown that even in 1949, when corporate saving was at a high level, individual saving accounted for about one-third of the total "new" savings available for investment. If the part of the saving attributed to unincorporated businesses that rather should be assigned as personal saving could be included in the calculation, the importance of the personal sector as a supplier of new funds for capital formation would appear even greater. Furthermore, it is evident that a relatively small number of family units headed largely by persons in the highest income quintile—a group with a heavy concentration of managerial and self-employed persons—account for the highest proportion of personal saving. Of the total of funds from individual saving in 1949, augmented by borrowed money and to some extent by the saving of unincorporated businesses, about two-thirds was applied to direct investment outlets such as purchase or construction of real estate, or capital expenditure by unincorporated business, and the remaining third to investments in financial assets.

The acquisition of financial assets by the personal sector represents the transference of funds to other sectors of the economy— the corporate sector and government. The financial assets of individuals are diverse, including types as different as currency, bank deposits, insurance, bonds, and corporate stocks. It is also apparent that such assets differ widely in their appeal to various strata of the population.

The following chapters will attempt to trace the ownership of certain types of financial assets by utilizing data on interest and dividend receipts obtained from a sample of the Wisconsin state income tax returns of individuals. The types of assets which can be traced from the tax returns include time deposits, savings and loan association shares, nonfederal debt obligations, and corporate stocks: assets that account for about one-half of the total of all financial assets held by the personal sector (excluding holdings of trust funds, financial institutions, etc.). By observing the distribution of those assets among different economic and social groups as shown by the sample, the analysis will provide, it is hoped, additional insight into the investment patterns of individuals.

CHAPTER 3

Use of Wisconsin Tax Returns for Estimates of Asset Holdings

The Sample

THE data on which this report is based are derived from a sample of Wisconsin state personal income tax returns for 1949. For that year returns were filed by individuals representing 1,018,333 families and single persons, and the number of persons dependent upon the reported income was 2,641,605, or 77.3 per cent of the total population of the state.[1] In general, Wisconsin residents are required to file returns if their net taxable income is $800 or more if single and $1,600 if married, or if they have total receipts of $5,000 or more. Since blank returns are mailed to those who have previously filed returns and to new names obtained from other sources, there are ordinarily a sizable number of returns filed on which no tax is payable.[2] Returns without tax were included in the sample when selected by chance from the parent population.

Total income for tax purposes in Wisconsin, as prescribed by regulations, is gross income less income tax-exempt under Wisconsin law and less allowable deductions, and is similar in most respects to the concept used by the Internal Revenue Service. The major exceptions important from our standpoint include the exemption of income from real estate located outside of Wisconsin, of interest received from federal government obligations, and of federal and state pensions (including pensions paid from the Wisconsin Teachers' Retirement Fund). Interest from state and local government obligations, however, is fully taxable, as are capital gains and losses regardless of how long the asset was held.

Notwithstanding the practice followed in most other studies, capital gains were included in the concept of income used in the present survey. Although they are frequently excluded from consumption studies, partly because of the belief that normally they do not enter into consumption expenditures, no such justification for

---

[1] Wisconsin Legislative Council, *1950 Report* (Madison, 1950), Vol. 1, pp. 374-75.

[2] For a detailed description of filing requirements and administrative practices, see "Income Size Distributions in the United States," *Studies in Income and Wealth, Volume Five*, Part II (National Bureau of Economic Research, 1943), pp. 5-36 to 5-39.

their exclusion can be made in a study of investment behavior. Furthermore, since income from capital gains is concentrated largely in the highest income groups, exclusion of this component would show a biased picture of the financial circumstances of at least some of the individuals in the sample.[3] A final reason for inclusion is that the special tax provisions affecting security transactions—a major source of capital gains—may have repercussions on individual investment practices.

Although the inclusion of capital gains in this instance gives a more appropriate concept of income, some less welcome effects must be noted. Including capital gains as part of income meant that some individuals had small or negative total incomes in 1949 when it was quite apparent that their reverses were only temporary. Similarly, in a few cases low income recipients in our sample were raised into the highest brackets by capital gains representing, for example, the sale of a family business or farm.

As defined for income tax purposes, total income in the state in 1949 was estimated to be $3,531 million—about 80 per cent of the $4,495 million total income payments to Wisconsin individuals in that year as estimated by the Department of Commerce.[4] The difference of $964 million is estimated to consist of $375 million of transfer payments, including interest on federal government bonds, $275 million of income received by individuals who received less than the amount required for filing, and $175 million representing late returns and additional income discovered by audit.[5] This would leave $139 million unaccounted for—presumably a measure of the underreporting present in the returns. However, the errors in the estimates are probably so great as to prevent the use of that figure in any but the roughest sense.

The filing exemption, as well as the concept of income used in the study, presents certain difficulties to obtaining data on the ownership of financial assets. Although returns are obtained from the great majority of income recipients and most of the total income received is reported, there is a small but probably significant group of individuals not filing returns who may be important holders of financial assets. Prominent among them may be individ-

[3] For a description of the distribution of capital gains among different income groups see *The Nature and Tax Treatment of Capital Gains and Losses*, by Lawrence H. Seltzer (National Bureau of Economic Research, 1951).

[4] *Survey of Current Business* (Department of Commerce), August 1950, Table 7, p. 19.

[5] Wisconsin Legislative Council, *op. cit.*, p. 335.

uals living largely on tax-exempt retirement incomes who receive rather sizable interest and dividend payments but in amounts under the minimum required for filing returns. In the analysis which follows, it will be understood that our data pertain only to persons who filed returns in 1949; unfortunately, there is no feasible method of obtaining information about the practices of persons who did not file returns.

A sample ultimately numbering 3,462 family units (some consisting of a single person, some representing a married couple only one of whom reported income, and some representing the joint information for a husband and wife who both had income) was selected from the universe of slightly over 1,000,000 tax returns. Only returns of individuals were selected; those of partnerships, corporations, and fiduciaries were excluded. Returns were sampled whether or not tax liability was indicated. The 3,462 units included in the sample had one common characteristic: they all reported interest or dividend income and thus evidenced individual ownership of financial assets. As has been indicated, the sampled returns were placed on a husband-wife basis; that is, whenever husband and wife filed separate returns—even though only one reported interest or dividend receipts—the incomes of both were combined in order to show the status of the unit as a whole. The income of additional persons in the family and data for estimating their investments were not obtained unless reported on the return of either husband or wife. For the sake of simplicity the term "individual" will be used for the units in the sample, as a means of referring to the investment holdings of individuals without constantly reiterating the presence of joint or combined, as well as single, returns in the evidence.

The only returns excluded after selection were those of a husband or wife whose spouse's return could not be located or those with gross unexplainable errors. A few returns, of course, did not itemize sources of interest and dividend income and therefore had to be omitted from the final sample.

The physical selection of the sample was not all that could have been desired, but perhaps the difficulties are not serious in effect. The returns were located in the four district offices of the Assessors of Income—Madison, Milwaukee, Appleton, and Eau Claire. The returns in each office had to be sampled during the interval after March 15 when they were available in an income sort as part of the processing procedure. Since it was not possible to run a continuous sample in each office as returns were processed, coverage differed as between offices. In all offices the returns had been sorted into three net taxable income groups ($0 to $4,999, $5,000 to $9,999, and $10,000 and over).[6] Because the returns were made available while divided into the three net taxable income groups, it was possible to make further income sorts based upon total instead of net taxable income and to apply sampling ratios such as would produce a sample heavily concentrated in the upper income groups —the most important investors. Returns were picked at set intervals to assure a random selection within any income group and tax district, although the sampling ratios varied among types of returns (long versus short forms), income groups, and different assessors' offices according to the coverage obtainable in the limited time that returns were available to the survey staff.

Differences in the coverage available within different assessors' offices and the resulting variation in sampling ratios for the several offices and for different income groups might have caused serious difficulty had it not been for the fact that control totals of income from interest and dividends were available from a survey of the same 1949 returns made by the research staff of the Wisconsin Legislative Council. A distribution of the interest and dividend income by total income groups for each tax district was obtained from that source. Since it was based on a random-stratified sample of approximately 100,000 returns, a much larger and technically more correct sample than was possible for the asset survey, the distribution of interest and dividend income among tax districts and among income groups within tax districts was presumably fairly representative of the total for the state and furnished benchmark data with which to correct unavoidable biases in the asset study.

The manner in which blow-up factors were computed in order to minimize biases arising from different sampling ratios for the several tax districts and income groups is shown in Table 6. As will be noted, all short forms and such long forms as reported negative income were treated separately and no distinction was made as to the office in which the return was filed. The long forms reporting positive income, however, were divided into two groups: those filed in the Milwaukee office and those filed in the other three offices. The latter grouping was thought desirable in order to eliminate the

[6] Net taxable income as defined by Wisconsin regulations differs from total income by allowable medical expenses, federal and state taxes, donations, dividends received from certain Wisconsin corporations, and minor items. While not taxable, dividends from firms doing half or more of their business within the state must be reported and itemized.

erratic behavior of cells containing only a few cases, and also to provide for separate weighting of these returns and of those filed in the more heavily populated district served by the Milwaukee office, where investment practices might be expected to be somewhat different. Column 1 of Table 6 gives an estimate of the interest and dividend receipts reported on the universe of all returns, derived from the 100,000-return sample, after adjustment to reflect the distribution of interest and dividend income in those cases in which married couples filing separate returns were considered as joint, instead of separate, income recipients. Column 2 was derived from the small sample of returns with interest and dividend information. The blow-up factors shown in column 3 represent the total estimated interest and dividend income on all returns divided by the total interest and dividend income on the sample returns for each income group within type of return class and administrative area.

The blow-up factors were used in three different ways: First, they were applied to the interest or dividend receipts of sampled individuals in order to estimate the total amount derived from various sources or received by various types of individuals. Second, they were applied to the estimated value of the asset holdings of individuals in the sample in order to show the estimated distribution of various types of asset holdings in value terms for the universe. Finally, they were used directly as an estimate of the number of individuals exhibiting a given characteristic or possessing a certain type of asset. While it might have been preferable to compute separate sets of blow-up factors for dollar amounts and for the number of individuals, card space and the time factor prevented doing so. Therefore blow-up factors for dollar amounts were also employed in the analysis involving number of individuals.

It should be noted that interest and dividend payments to owners of the types of assets covered in the present survey do not account for all interest and dividend payments reported by individuals on their tax returns. As shown in Table 6, interest and dividend receipts reported by taxpayers in 1949 amounted to $132.8 million. In contrast, only $127.5 million is estimated to result from the ownership of the types of financial assets covered in the survey. The discrepancy between the two figures is accounted for by the fact that in editing the returns the following types of receipts were eliminated: misplaced wage and salary, rent, or fiduciary items; interest (and in some cases principal) received from federal government obligations erroneously reported; interest and dividends

ESTIMATING ASSETS FROM TAX RETURNS

TABLE 6

Derivation of Blow-up Factors for Estimating Asset Holdings of Wisconsin Individuals from Sampled Tax Returns

	INTEREST AND DIVIDEND INCOME		
DISTRICT, TYPE OF RETURN, AND TOTAL INCOME GROUP	All Returns[a] (000)	Sample Returns[b]	Blow-up Factors[c]
ALL DISTRICTS			
Short Form	$5,742	$33,186	...
$0-999	610	3,006	202.9
1,000-1,999	1,408	6,537	215.4
2,000-2,999	1,641	9,933	165.2
3,000-3,999	1,039	7,090	146.5
4,000-4,999	763	5,105	149.5
5,000 and over	281	1,515	185.5
Long Form—Negative Income	4,375	51,822	84.4
MILWAUKEE DISTRICT			
Long Form—Positive Income	63,530	8,424,082	...
$0-999	820	4,095	200.2
1,000-1,999	2,640	19,073	138.4
2,000-2,999	2,681	32,854	81.6
3,000-3,999	2,674	26,085	102.5
4,000-4,999	3,666	27,045	135.6
5,000-9,999	10,122	197,664	51.2
10,000-19,999	11,258	485,918	23.2
20,000-49,999	14,407	1,200,017	12.0
50,000 and over	15,262	6,431,331	2.3
MADISON, APPLETON, EAU CLAIRE DISTRICTS			
Long Form—Positive Income	59,193	8,170,853	...
$0-999	1,440	16,682	86.3
1,000-1,999	3,538	46,097	76.8
2,000-2,999	5,714	63,816	89.5
3,000-3,999	3,924	39,739	98.7
4,000-4,999	5,103	36,517	139.7
5,000-9,999	12,113	295,862	40.9
10,000-19,999	8,151	615,724	13.2
20,000-49,999	9,275	1,070,948	8.7
50,000 and over	9,935	5,985,468	1.7
All Forms	$132,840	$16,679,943	...

[a] Estimated from a sample of 100,000 Wisconsin tax returns for 1949 made by the Wisconsin Legislative Council. Sample data on interest and dividend income of husbands and wives filing separate returns have been adjusted to reflect their distribution on a joint return basis.

[b] Represents the distribution of interest and dividend income by total income groups for the sample of 3,462 tax returns (single returns, or joint or combined returns of husband and wife who both reported income) giving usable asset information.

[c] Computed by dividing the estimated total of interest and dividend income for all returns by the amount of such income reported on sample returns.

from insurance policies; cooperative association stock dividends; liquidating dividends, and stock dividends.[7] While in numerous cases these items were subtracted by the taxpayer before determining his income for tax purposes, they were included in the tabulations from which the blown-up distributions of interest and dividend income were made and thus had to be carried in the sample distribution to compute the necessary blow-up factors.

Method of Valuing Asset Holdings

The information reported in the Wisconsin income tax returns on interest and dividend receipts of individuals was sufficient to determine holdings of three broad types of asset: deposit assets—time deposits, savings and loan association shares, and the like (termed for present purposes "time deposits and related claims"); direct debt instruments such as bonds and notes; and corporate stocks. The assets held were valued either by capitalizing their incomes at typical rates prevailing in Wisconsin in 1949, or by using the 1949 prices of each issue of bonds and stocks for which specific information could be obtained. Either method gives an estimate of the average value of holdings during 1949 rather than of the amount held at a particular date in that year. The following sections describe the methods used in valuing specific types of assets within the three broad groups.

TIME DEPOSITS AND RELATED CLAIMS

Most investment incomes reported on Wisconsin tax returns were payments to depositors by time departments of commercial banks, mutual savings banks, the postal savings system, credit unions, and savings and loan associations. In estimating the dollar volume of deposits owned by individuals in the sample, typical 1949 rates paid by Wisconsin institutions were used as capitalization ratios rather than specific rates paid by each bank, savings and loan association, or other institution.

The typical stated rate paid by the time departments of commercial banks during 1949 was 1 per cent; but there is reason to believe that capitalization at that rate would underestimate deposit amounts in a good many cases. Many banks compute interest on only a part of the total savings account or for only a part of the time funds are on deposit, if they are withdrawn between interest

[7] Also excluded were interest and dividend receipts not itemized by specific source but instead attributed to nominees or to brokers and dealers. Fortunately, most individuals holding securities in such manner itemized the receipts by source as required by law.

payment dates. Accordingly, the effective rate would actually be less than 1 per cent.

A sample survey made in 1947 by the American Bankers Association showed that in that year 34 out of 57 Wisconsin banks computed interest in such a manner that a 1 per cent stated rate yielded an effective rate of 0.86 per cent.[8] This checked closely with the average effective rate of 0.85 per cent paid in 1949 by all insured commercial banks in Wisconsin, which was based on average balance sheet figures and on expenditure figures for 1949 on interest payments to time depositors. Time deposit income from commercial banks was therefore capitalized at 0.85 per cent.

Similarly, average effective rates for Wisconsin institutions were used to capitalize the dividends from savings and loan associations and credit unions, which were estimated to yield 2.84 and 2.46 per cent, respectively, on the basis of combined balance sheets and operating statements of all chartered institutions located in Wisconsin. Interest receipts from postal savings accounts were capitalized at the standard 2.00 per cent rate, and the few from mutual savings banks at the same rate.

DIRECT DEBT ASSETS (BONDS, NOTES, ETC.)

Four types of direct debt instruments were distinguishable: traded corporate and foreign government bonds; state, county, and municipal tax-exempt bonds; notes and mortgages of individuals; and notes, bonds, and other debt obligations of business organizations normally not traded through organized channels. Holdings of U.S. savings bonds and other federal government bonds were not included, since interest receipts from that source are not taxable in Wisconsin.

The first group—termed here traded bonds—were valued individually by capitalizing the interest payment received from a particular issue at the coupon rate shown in the investment manuals.[9] Thus, $100 of interest received from the Chicago and Erie Railroad was considered to represent $2,000 in principal value, since the one bond issue of that company carried a coupon rate of 5 per cent.[10] The principal value was then adjusted to the un-

---

[8] Information furnished by the Savings Division of the American Bankers Association.

[9] A substantial number of the interest payments received from corporate bonds were not multiples of the coupon rate because of the deduction of bank collection charges, but these charges were taken into account in the valuation process.

[10] The method of identifying and valuing bonds of corporations with two or more issues was the same as that used in the case of stocks of corporations with more than one issue, discussed in the next subsection.

weighted mean between the high and the low market price for 1949. The market value of the above-mentioned holding was thus estimated at $2,444, based on the unweighted mean market price of 122.2 for 1949. For a small number of foreign bond issues no information could be obtained, and it was therefore necessary to estimate their market value by capitalizing the reported income from them at 4.18 per cent, which was the ratio of interest payment to market price for the foreign bonds on which information was available.

It proved impossible to value the issues of larger governmental units at market price because so many had identical coupon rates but matured at widely different and often unidentifiable dates. Therefore they were valued individually by capitalizing the reported income receipts at their coupon rate; that is, they were valued at par instead of at market. Data were lacking altogether on a number of issues of smaller governmental units, which were therefore valued at a 2.5 per cent capitalization rate—the ratio between estimated face value and interest payment for such issues as could be identified. All direct debt obligations of individuals and business firms on which no data could be obtained were valued by capitalization at a uniform 5 per cent rate.[11]

CORPORATE STOCKS

Corporations may be divided on the basis of breadth of stock ownership into two groups: the large corporations which generally raise external capital by the issuance of stock to the general public, and the much more numerous corporations which finance themselves by stock sales to a few individuals. Closely held corporate shares are seldom traded and for the most part remain in the hands of the families originally associated with the business. The distinction is one of degree, of course, but it must be recognized in determining the value of stockholdings.

In valuing stockholdings, publicly owned issues were distinguished from closely held issues by determining, from the file of stock issues held by individuals in the sample, all issues upon

[11] In view of the low interest rates prevailing in 1949, 6 per cent would probably have been too high; and while bank loans at 4 per cent might have been available for some of the better quality borrowers, many of the loans held by individuals might not have been desirable paper for commercial banks. In the Seventh Federal Reserve District in 1946 the average rate on business loans to borrowers with assets of less than $50,000, charged by member banks with deposits of less than $2 million, was 5.3 per cent. See "The Structure of Interest Rates on Business Loans at Member Banks," by Richard Youngdahl, *Federal Reserve Bulletin*, July 1947, Table 14, p. 815.

which information on dividends and market prices for 1949 could be obtained. From the published investment manuals stock issues with 1949 price and dividend quotations were segregated and labeled "traded stocks"; the stock issues without price quotations or dividend information were labeled "untraded stocks." It should be borne in mind that the distinction between traded and untraded stocks is not precisely the distinction between publicly held issues and closely held issues, although for most purposes the correspondence is high.

Traded Stocks. Traded stock was valued in the following manner. The dividends reported on a tax return, divided by the 1949 dividend rate on the particular issue held, gave an estimate of the average number of shares of that issue held by the individual in 1949. The number of shares when multiplied by the unweighted mean between the high and the low 1949 market price gave an approximate market value. Thus, a $90.00 dividend payment from the American Telephone and Telegraph Company was determined to represent a holding of ten shares of stock, since the dividend rate in 1949 was $9.00 per share. At the unweighted mean price between the 1949 high of 155⅜ and the 1949 low of 146¼, namely 150.9, the value of such a holding was estimated at $1,509.[12]

It was more difficult to value the stocks of corporations with more than one issue. Whenever the individual receiving dividends from such a company did not specify the type of issue (that is, whether preferred or common), the holding was regarded as the issue whose annual dividend rate, when divided into the total dividend payment received by the taxpayer, yielded a computed number of shares in even multiples or fractions of 100.[13]

---

[12] In a number of instances the reported dividend receipt differed from the annual dividend per share shown in the investment manuals, and some adjustment had to be made in the dividend rate in order to estimate correctly the value of the security. For example, dividends received from corporations paying the Wisconsin dividend tax were most frequently reported after deduction of the tax, whereas dividend rates were, of course, reported before deduction. Dividends from Canadian and other foreign corporations were frequently reported after deduction of a nonresident tax and after conversion into United States dollars, while the dividends given in manuals were not so adjusted. In one case, dividends from a foreign corporation were also subject to a progressive income tax, for which adjustment had to be made. The dividend rates of a large number of investment trust holdings had to be adjusted because some taxpayers reported dividends before deduction of capital gains distributions while others reported their dividend receipts after such deductions.

[13] Thus, a dividend payment of $37.50 from the General Motors Corporation might have represented payment on 4.69 shares of common stock at $8.00 per share, 7.5 shares of $5.00 cumulative preferred stock, or 10 shares of $3.75 cumulative preferred stock. Such a case would be resolved in favor of the $3.75 preferred stock. Similarly, if the total dividends reported from General

Since the method of valuation, here and for the other types of asset, gave an average holding for 1949 rather than a holding as of a particular date during the year, its result would be inaccurate in the case of an individual whose holdings were bought or sold during the year. For instance, a $225.00 dividend payment from the American Telephone and Telegraph Company could have represented payment of dividends on 25 shares held during the entire year, 100 shares held for one quarter, or 50 shares held for two quarters, since the dividend paid per quarter was $2.25 per share. Because it was impossible to determine whether a reported issue was purchased during 1949, it was assumed that the combined holdings of all individuals in the sample (or any subgroup of the sample) remained constant, though the holdings of any individual in the sample might change. Although the sales price of stock sold during the year was available from the capital gains schedule of the tax returns, these stocks were valued in most of the tabulations by capitalizing dividends received from them at the yearly rate for the sake of consistency with the above procedure.[14] Only in tabulations showing the measurement of sales volume were stocks sold during the year valued at actual sales price.

Untraded Stocks. Three alternatives were considered in selecting a method of measuring the investment of individuals in corporations whose stock is seldom traded: first, the relative importance of these assets might have been measured by the estimated amount of dividends derived from them; second, dividends from untraded stocks might have been capitalized at some specified rate of return; and third, the book value of the stocks could have been determined. In one or two important comparisons of holdings of traded and untraded stocks, the first method was employed; that is,

---

Motors had been $40.00, the holdings would have been classified as 5 shares of common stock rather than as 8 shares of $5.00 preferred stock or 10.67 shares of $3.75 preferred stock.

In some cases the dividend payments per share on two or more different issues were even multiples of each other or were identical. Thus, $300.00 received from the Coca-Cola Corporation might have represented dividend payments on 50 shares of common stock paying $6.00 per share, or 100 shares of $3.00 Class A stock. Since the corporation had about seven times as many shares of common stock outstanding as of Class A stock, individuals' dividend receipts were distributed arbitrarily by classifying one out of every seven such holdings at random as Class A stock and calling the remainder common stock.

[14] Valuation at the reported sales price would have involved double counting. Suppose investor X has $1,000 which he invests in stock A at the beginning of the year. He receives one quarterly dividend, sells the stock for $1,000, and invests it in stock B, repeating the process each quarter. A valuation at sale price would credit him with a holding of $1,000 in each of the four stocks, or $4,000. Valuation by capitalizing at the annual rate would credit him with a holding of $250 in each of the four stocks, or $1,000, as his average holding for the year.

dividend income was used to contrast the relative importance of traded and untraded issues. That method was not generally used, however, because it did not provide value measurements—one of the principal aims of the study. On the other hand, the capitalization method of valuing untraded stocks seemed unsuitable because it would have involved arbitrary selection of a specified rate of return that would give a reasonable indication of the risk premium adhering to investment in closely held corporations. The third and most convenient alternative, valuation of corporation stocks at book value, would involve substantial errors; yet it was adopted because it was the only method of obtaining value information which avoided tenuous assumptions about the risk question.

Nearly all of the untraded stocks in the sample were issues of Wisconsin corporations or of companies doing a sizable share of their total business in that state. They were valued at book on the basis of information obtained from the Wisconsin corporate income tax returns of the corporations in question. The ratio between the dividend receipt reported by the individual in the sample and all dividends paid by a particular corporation was applied to the book value of the corporation as of the balance sheet date nearest to December 31, 1949, giving the pro rata share of the particular corporation's total book value attributable to the individual stockholder. The identification of preferred and common issues was handled in the same manner as for traded securities.

Some dividends were received from closely held corporations filing no tax returns in Wisconsin and in most instances not doing business within the state. In order to value the holdings of their stocks, it was necessary to assume that there was no important difference in rate of return (annual dividends divided by book value) between corporations for which information was available and those for which no data were obtainable from tax sources. Therefore, stocks of the latter were valued by capitalizing reported dividends at the same rate as that earned on the stocks of closely held corporations for which an estimate of book value could be obtained.

In one respect, however, the application of across-the-board capitalization rates as just described would have introduced a bias, since many of the closely held corporations whose book value could be ascertained were local banks whereas most of the "nonidentifiable" corporations were out-of-state nonbank companies. For that reason two ratios were computed for valuing the unidentified stocks: one for nonbank corporation stocks, the other for bank stocks. Unidentified nonbank stocks were valued by capitalizing dividends at the rate of 5.20 per cent. The comparable figure for bank stocks was 2.44 per cent.

The use of book value to measure the amount of untraded stocks involves two sources of error when comparisons are made with the market value of traded stocks. In general, the book value of corporate stock in 1949 was greater than its market value, so that the use of unadjusted book value as a measure for untraded stock holdings tended to overstate their importance in relation to traded corporate stocks. Rough estimates of the book value of corporate stocks in all industry groups at the beginning of 1949, and of their market value at the end of the year, indicated that the market value was something like 70 per cent of the book value.[15] More important is the fact that corporations differ greatly in the relation of the book to the market value of their securities and that book value itself appears subject to fluctuations arising from conventional methods of corporate accounting which do not take into account unrealized changes in the value of corporation-owned assets. While the ratio of market to book value for bank stocks appears fairly consistent throughout the banking industry—between 80 and 90 per cent, with only a few cases in which market exceeds book value—that is not true for nonbank stocks. Not only is there considerably greater variation in the ratio of market to book value in the case of nonbank corporation stocks, but the book value of the stocks of small nonbank corporations frequently exceeds the market value, sometimes by as much as 100 per cent. The average ratio of market to book value for corporations other than railroads and financial corporations including banks was roughly 74 per cent in 1949.[16]

The estimated book value of untraded stocks held by individuals in different income groups was adjusted to a market value equivalent as in Table A-2 by applying 0.87 to the book value of bank stocks and 0.74 to the book value of nonbank stocks. This adjustment, while necessarily crude, seemed worth while in order to correct for the overvaluation of untraded as compared with traded stocks. The result of the adjustment is to reduce the amount of untraded stocks held by any given group of investors below that shown by the unadjusted book value. Holdings of the lowest income groups

---

[15] Raymond W. Goldsmith and Alexander Ganz, "Estimate of Market Value of Corporate Stock: 1900-1949" (National Bureau of Economic Research, Capital Requirements Study, Work Memorandum 32, mimeographed, December 1951), Table 21, p. 64.

[16] Ibid., Table 21, p. 64.

are reduced somewhat less than the holdings of the highest income groups, because of the concentration of bank stocks in the lower income groups. Most of the analysis of Chapters 4 and 5 is based on a market value equivalent concept in valuing untraded stocks. Some evidence may be seen in Table 21 that to use the unadjusted book value of untraded stocks instead does not materially alter the analysis, except when aggregate amounts of traded and untraded stocks are compared.

From Tables A-1, A-2, and A-3 it may be calculated that the yield on traded stock in the sample amounts to 6.6 per cent (Moody's average dividend yield for 200 stocks in 1949 was 6.63 per cent) and the yield on untraded stock to 6.3 per cent based on market value equivalent. It has been suggested by numerous readers that the yield on untraded stock should be higher than the yield on traded stock, presumably because of the greater risk attached to holdings of untraded stock in small corporations. Yet in 1949 even in the case of marketed stocks, those issues with the three poorest agency rating grades (CCC, CC, and C) yielded less than medium or B grade stocks (see Chart 16). Furthermore, there is no proof that the untraded stocks were any riskier than stocks of corporations with issues traded on the exchanges.

Coverage of the Survey

The survey estimates of the financial assets held by individuals are necessarily restricted by the nature of the data employed: they are restricted geographically and to only certain types of assets, and they are subject to the limitations, such as incomplete reporting, which characterize tax data.

The geographic restriction is probably no more than a minor difficulty in a cross-section survey. In most economic measures Wisconsin ranks about midway in the array of states, and presumably the investment practices of its citizens do not vary greatly from those of individuals in a large group of states which are neither predominantly industrial nor predominantly agricultural in composition. While geographic peculiarities in investment practices doubtless exist, such basic trends as the relation of income level to stockholdings are probably broadly similar for the country as a whole, even though in one region individuals at a given income level may hold more stocks than individuals with comparable incomes living in another section of the country.

As was shown in Table 5, approximately one-half of the estimated value of all financial assets held by individuals is attributable to types covered in the survey of Wisconsin income tax returns. The important omissions are cash and demand deposits, federal government bonds, the asset value of life insurance, bonds and other debt instruments in default, and stock of corporations which paid no dividends in 1949. The survey also excludes rental property, mineral and timber leaseholds, and the value of ownership interests in unincorporated businesses. The omitted types of assets were probably more important in the lower than in the higher income groups, so that care should be exercised in using the survey results to show differences in relative wealth position of various groups in 1949.[17]

In estimating the total amount of interest and dividend income not reported because of filing exemptions and underreporting, estimates for the United States as a whole had to be used. Because such estimates are derived from small samples, they are of somewhat dubious accuracy when applied to a particular region. The Department of Commerce has estimated that 60 per cent of all nonfederal cash-interest payments and 33 per cent of all corporate dividends received in 1947 by individuals in the United States were not reported on federal income tax returns for that year.[18] These underreporting ratios may be applied to estimated total cash-interest and corporate dividend payments made to Wisconsin residents in 1949 (exclusive of federal interest payments), and the result compared with the amount actually reported on state income tax returns.

The Department of Commerce estimated that $146 million in corporate dividends and $85 million in nonfederal cash-interest payments were received by Wisconsin residents in 1949. Two-thirds of the former and a somewhat lower proportion of the latter —probably only two-fifths—would be expected to appear on federal income tax returns. In all, $131.4 million of the estimated interest and dividend receipts might appear on the federal returns. Actually, $132.8 million of interest and dividend income was reported on

[17] See "The Pattern of Estate Tax Wealth," by Horst Mendershausen (Life Insurance Association of America, Saving and Capital Market Study, Advisory Committee Memorandum No. 29, mimeographed, unpublished, February 1950), Table 23, p. 99.

[18] Information furnished by National Income Division, Office of Business Economics, Department of Commerce. The discrepancy, of course, does not indicate the extent of tax evasion on interest and dividend income, because not all interest and dividends are taxable or received by persons required to file returns.

Wisconsin state income tax returns for 1949, as was shown in Table 6.[19]

The comparison indicates that the Wisconsin tax returns experience virtually the same degree of underreporting of investment income as do federal tax returns. There is some evidence to show, furthermore, that corrections for comparability reduce the underreporting of dividends from 33 per cent to around 24 per cent.[20] This fact is not particularly comforting, however, because in any case the interest and dividend income which is unaccounted for is a large part of the total and there is no direct evidence as to whether, in the case of Wisconsin returns, the missing income is distributed proportionately to the distribution of that actually reported or whether underreporting is more prevalent in one income group than in another.

Material derived from the Federal Audit Control Program of 1948, however, does show the areas of greatest underreporting on federal returns, and this may be relevant. Unpublished (and necessarily very rough) estimates, made at the National Bureau of Economic Research by Daniel M. Holland, suggest that underreporting of both interest and dividends is relatively greater the lower the income class of the taxpayer. His estimates indicate also that underreporting is probably more prevalent in the case of interest than it is in the case of dividend receipts.

If underreporting of income from financial assets on Wisconsin income tax returns is similar in character to that found in the federal income tax returns, the survey estimates have smaller downward bias in the case of dividend-bearing assets than in the case of interest-bearing assets. It follows also that the low income segments of the population have substantially more financial assets than they are credited with in the tables. For that reason little emphasis is placed on the distribution of assets among different income groups; most of the analysis consists of comparisons of the composition of financial asset holdings at various income levels. In final analysis the apparent biases appear to strengthen the major

---

[19] There are some minor inaccuracies in the comparison. The state total includes federal interest erroneously reported and state and local bond interest, while the federal total excludes interest from state and local bonds. The state total excludes fiduciaries, nonprofit organizations, and partnerships, but the federal total includes them.

[20] See "Appraisal of Basic Data Available for Constructing Income Size Distributions," by Selma F. Goldsmith, in *Conference on Research in Income and Wealth, Volume Thirteen* (National Bureau of Economic Research, 1951), Table 8, p. 302, for the 1946 ratio of reported dividends to adjusted estimate of dividends received.

conclusions of the study, for a predominance of interest-bearing obligations in the lowest income groups is found, even without correction for differential underreporting of receipts. Accordingly, it was thought best not to make corrections for underreporting.

More direct checks on the accuracy of the data can be made in connection with interest and dividend payments on types of assets for which total payments are known. It is estimated, for instance, that only about 35 per cent of the commercial bank interest on savings accounts actually paid or credited during 1949 was reported on the Wisconsin tax returns. Since some interest payments on time deposits were made to other than individuals, underreporting in the survey data, though large, would probably be less than that figure implies. In contrast, nearly 60 per cent of the total amount of dividends paid by Wisconsin savings and loan associations is estimated to have been reported on tax returns.

A comparison of estimated and actual total dollar values of individual holdings of time deposits in banks, savings and loan associations, and credit unions as shown by the 1946 Survey of Liquid Assets reveals that the personal interview method, which was employed in the survey, gives results for the entire nation which are from 55 to 65 per cent complete in the categories mentioned.[21] In contrast, the estimate of total interest and dividends received from those sources based on the sample of Wisconsin tax returns appears to be only 45 to 50 per cent complete.[22]

The final evaluation of the advantages of studying financial asset holdings on the basis of data taken from income tax returns must be relative. Can better results be achieved by any other feasible method? A comparison of the results derived from the analysis of tax returns with those of personal interview surveys appears to favor the former in the categories which are important for studying financial asset holdings, namely, interest and dividend receipts. Estimates of interest and dividend income based on the results of the joint survey by the Bureau of Labor Statistics and the Bureau of Human Nutrition and Home Economics for 1941, the census surveys for 1944 and 1945, and the survey by the Bureau of the Census and the Bureau of Agricultural Economics for 1946 disclosed no more than 16 to 32 per cent of the totals estimated

[21] "A National Survey of Liquid Assets," *Federal Reserve Bulletin*, June 1946, p. 580.
[22] The approximate ratio given does not take into consideration the fact that some time deposits are held by individuals not filing tax returns.

ESTIMATING ASSETS FROM TAX RETURNS

by the National Income Division of the Department of Commerce.[23] By comparison, 40 per cent of nonfederal cash-interest income and 66 per cent of dividend income showed up on federal tax returns in 1947, and similar amounts on the 1949 Wisconsin tax returns. Thus, while income tax returns have definite limitations as source material for data on financial asset holdings, experience has shown that they account for more of the receipts from investments than do the usual interview surveys and therefore would be subject to smaller areas of uncertainty.

[23] Selma F. Goldsmith, *op. cit.*, Table 3, pp. 288-89.

CHAPTER 4

The Relation between Income Status and the Pattern of Investment

THE first task of the analysis is to determine how the ownership of various types of financial assets is related to the personal income structure. There are two facets to such an inquiry, both of which are important in explaining the composition and distribution of asset ownership. Proportionately more persons in a high income group may own a particular type of asset than in a low income group; frequency of ownership, in other words, may be a function of income. Also, the dollar amount of holdings of different types of asset may vary systematically according to the income levels of individuals.

In the present inquiry the major aim in relating income to asset ownership—that is, to investment preference patterns—is to determine how savings are allocated at different income levels between equity and debt assets and between direct and indirect forms of debt obligations. For purposes of inferring the relation between income level and the manner of investing current savings, we look at the composition of financial asset holdings at different income levels. If savings are largely channeled into time deposits and related claims through financial intermediaries, important problems arise as to the manner in which these institutions invest their funds. If savers prefer debt rather than equity claims as an outlet for their savings, while the users of savings are inclined to avoid high debt ratios, other problems arise.

In relating income levels to investment preference patterns as revealed in a cross-section of asset holdings, we are observing only indirectly the process by which current savings are channeled into investment. Even if we could discover how the individuals in the sample chose to allocate their 1949 savings, and if this were related to their income levels, there would still be considerable doubt as to the true effect of income size on the pattern of individual investment preferences. The financial investments which many individuals hold may bear only an incidental relationship to their present or past economic status, and the form in which some or all of their accumulated savings are held may be the result of quite unrelated circumstances.

Three factors other than income which may account for the types of assets which individuals hold appear significant. First, some assets may accrue to individuals through inheritance or in settlement of debts, and their retention in the same form may be involuntary in the sense that the owner may be reluctant to accept an apparent loss. Second, some individuals through their occupational attachments are more favorably situated to make certain investments than are others. For example, lawyers and bankers may have more opportunities to invest in small corporations than do doctors or teachers. Third, individuals differ in their familiarity with various types of investments: for instance, corporate managers and accountants probably have a higher regard for corporate stocks than do farmers or owners of other unincorporated businesses. Some other reasons for what may be termed "derived" investments—that is, assets acquired more or less as an incident to some special circumstance, in contrast to those deliberately selected with regard to their own merits from a broad range of alternative investments—are discussed in later chapters. Here it will suffice to observe that the operation of the responsible factors tends to obscure the relationship between income and investment preferences and introduces some degree of spurious correlation into the analysis. In the next chapter, for example, it is observed that managerial and self-employed persons (except farmers) are important holders of corporate stocks. Since managers and self-employed persons as a group have higher than average incomes, one cannot be sure what effect income level alone, as against occupational status, has upon the type of financial assets owned. One would have to consider the fact that significant differences in the occupations of persons composing the several income groups may account for the observed differences in types of assets held at various income levels. These are some of the problems encountered in trying, by an examination of the current holdings of financial assets by income groups, to infer the relation between income level and the direction in which current savings are channeled.

In addition to throwing light upon the sources of investment funds, information as to who owns particular types of assets is important in our general knowledge of finance. For example, a distribution of the dollar value of particular types of assets among different income groups enables one to say that, on the basis of the evidence, proportionately more of the value of asset A is owned by the lowest income group (under $5,000) than of the value of asset B. While such matters are of no more than moderate interest to the economist, they are of very great practical value to the financial community which must grapple with the problems of selling financial assets. One section of this chapter, therefore, concerns the distribution of financial assets among income groups.

For reasons that will become evident, the conclusions on the distribution of financial assets among income groups are couched in rather general terms. The statistics are not completely free from ambiguities; beyond that, none of the distributions derived from either tax or interview survey data account for the sum total of particular types of assets known to be in the hands of individuals, as was seen in Chapter 3. It is evident that conclusions regarding the distribution of the dollar value of particular types of asset, therefore, rest on the assumption that the missing quantity of the financial asset is distributed in exactly the same manner as is the known quantity. In Chapter 3, some reason was indicated for doubting that assumption. Nevertheless, the major conclusions drawn from the distribution of assets among income groups are instructive.

Finally, it is clear that lines of cause-and-effect relationships run both ways between income and financial asset ownership. The last section explores some of the facets of that topic.

The Relation between Income and Financial Asset Ownership

The relation between personal income level and the ownership of financial assets may best be described as a product of two separate but related phenomena. On the one hand, the proportion of individuals holding a particular asset may differ substantially for different levels of income. In other words, frequency of ownership would be expected to vary not only as between types of assets at all income levels, but also as between income levels even for a single type of asset. On the other hand, the typical or average size of holding of a particular asset is also likely to differ as between income groups. Together, frequency of ownership and size of holding of a particular asset underlie more general aspects of the relation between income and the ownership of financial assets.

FREQUENCY OF OWNERSHIP

Caution is necessary in interpreting data from tax returns on the frequency of ownership of financial assets. Many persons may forget or intentionally omit the reporting of minor amounts of interest and dividend receipts on their tax returns; while the dollar value of such assets may be small, the number of holders of such unreported assets may be a significant proportion of the total number of holders. It will be observed in Table 7 that Wisconsin taxpayers reporting some type of savings account

TABLE 7

Estimated Frequency of Ownership of Specified Types of Financial Asset by Wisconsin Individuals, 1949

Type of Asset	Number of Holders	As Percentage of All Income Units[a]
Some financial assets[b]	209,652	19.0%
Time deposits and related claims	135,743	12.3
Direct debt assets	66,230	6.0
Some corporate stock[c]	93,281	8.5
Traded stock	72,000	6.5
Untraded stock	46,189	4.2

Based on survey of tax returns, with returns of husband and wife both reporting income converted to a joint basis if not already so.

[a] Based on the number of income units in Wisconsin—1,102,380 families and single persons—given in the *1950 Census of Population*, Vol. 2, Part 49, Wisconsin, Chapter B, Table 32, p. 49.

[b] The number of holders of some financial asset of the types specified is less than the sum of the number of holders for all types because some individuals held more than one type.

[c] The number of holders of corporate stock is less than the sum of the number of holders of traded plus untraded stock because some individuals held stock of both types.

in 1949 appeared to make up about 12 per cent of all income units. This figure is considerably lower than that estimated on the basis of the 1949 Survey of Consumer Finances, where it was found that 44 per cent of all spending units owned one or more assets classified as savings deposits.[1] The discrepancy may be due to the tendency of many individuals, when making out their tax returns, to forget or to ignore the small amounts of income derived from savings accounts. It may be significant, nevertheless, that the returns indicated that approximately twice as many individuals held some form of indirect debt instrument (time deposits and the like) as held direct debt instruments (bonds, mortgages, etc.).

[1] "1949 Survey of Consumer Finances," *Federal Reserve Bulletin*, October 1949, p. 1197.

INCOME STATUS AND INVESTMENT

Holders of some type of corporate stock, either traded or untraded, apparently numbered 8.5 per cent of the total estimated income units; but the figure might be considerably larger if a correction were made for underreporting and to include holders who did not file and holders of stock which did not pay dividends in 1949. The estimate of the frequency of holders of traded issues —6.5 per cent of all units in Wisconsin—may be compared with the nationwide estimate for 1949 made by the Survey of Consumer Finances that 8 per cent of all spending units owned stock in corporations open to investment by the general public.[2]

There is some evidence that the frequency of stock ownership in Wisconsin in 1949 was quite close to that for the United States as a whole. A survey of the geographic distribution of holders of 494 over-the-counter stocks (excluding mutual funds) was made by the National Association of Securities Dealers in 1951.[3] The gross number of stockholders found in each state was compared with the total population for that state, though no attempt was made to correct for the fact that some holders had stock in two or more corporations. The comparable percentage figures, as computed in that survey, were 1.388 per cent for Wisconsin and 1.276 per cent for the United States as a whole.

In comparison to about 7 per cent for the holdings of traded stock issues, only about 4 per cent of the Wisconsin individuals sampled held stock in corporations whose equity securities were not traded on exchanges or in the organized over-the-counter market (Table 7). It may be added that the practice of holding both traded and untraded issues appears to have been considerably more prevalent in the higher than in the lower income groups, where it was more frequent for stock owners to hold either one type or the other.

The relationship between income and frequency of ownership for the four types of asset on which ownership data are available from the survey of Wisconsin tax returns is shown in Chart 1. Only three different income ranges are used because the total number of units in the various income groups is based on the 1950 population census, which did not provide detailed estimates above the $10,000 income level.[4] In spite of that limitation, frequency

[2] *Ibid.*, p. 1190.
[3] *1951 Stockholders-Distribution Survey*, Release of National Association of Securities Dealers, August 27, 1951, p. 2.
[4] Unless otherwise indicated, the classification of income levels as lower, middle, or upper used in this and subsequent chapters refers to the following class

INCOME STATUS AND INVESTMENT

of ownership of the various types of asset is observed to vary systematically with income, with some types showing greater variation than others. Frequency of ownership of time deposits and related claims changes least with income status, while frequency of ownership of direct debt assets shows a somewhat greater change with income level. It is the proportion of individuals holding some amount of corporate stock that shows the greatest increase as higher income groups are considered.

What about types of financial assets not covered by the Wis-

CHART 1

Estimated Frequency of Ownership of Specified Types of Financial Asset, 1949, for Income Groups of Wisconsin Individuals

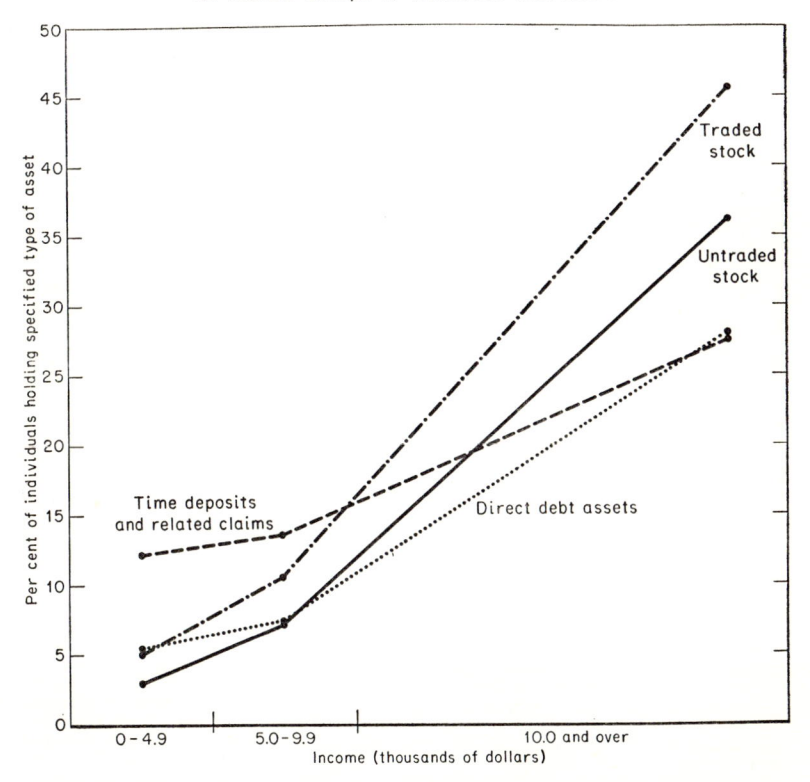

Based on Table A-5, and on number of families and single persons in Wisconsin given in Census of Population: 1950, Vol. 2, Part 49, Wisconsin, Chapter B, Table 32, p. 49.
Readings are centered at midpoints of income class intervals, except that for the $10,000 and over class the approximate mean, $23,000, is used.

intervals: lower, $0 to $4,999; middle, $5,000 to $9,999; and upper, $10,000 and over.

consin data? Chart 2 shows the frequency of ownership of checking accounts and U.S. savings bonds (Series A to F) as disclosed by the Survey of Consumer Finances for early 1950, and the frequency of ownership of life insurance as shown by the 1951 survey. These estimates cover the entire United States and differ somewhat from the Wisconsin material in that spending units are the basis of the data. Furthermore, because tax and interview data differ in their inherent biases, the figures on frequency of ownership of the assets mentioned are not directly comparable with the Wisconsin data for other types of asset.

CHART 2

Estimated Frequency of Ownership of Specified Types of Financial Asset, for Income Groups of Spending Units in the United States

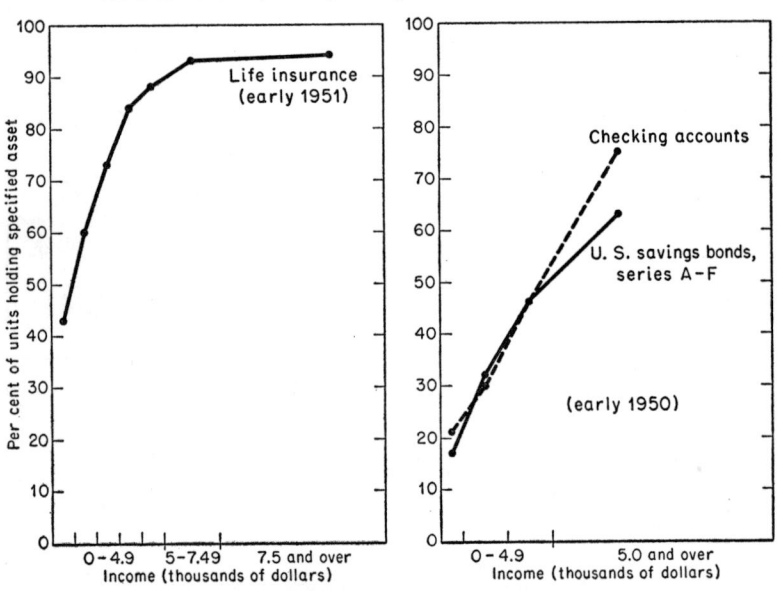

From Survey of Consumer Finances data for checking accounts and United States savings bonds in Federal Reserve Bulletin, December 1950, Table 9, p. 1593, and for life insurance in the Bulletin of December 1951, Table 15, p. 1526.

Readings are centered at midpoints of income class intervals except that for open-end classes the approximate mean is used: $8,000 for owners of checking accounts and savings bonds with incomes of $5,000 and over; $12,500 for owners of life insurance with incomes of $7,500 and over.

As is the case with time deposits and related claims, direct debt, and corporate equities, the frequency of ownership of life insurance, checking accounts, and U.S. savings bonds increases with income level. The smallest change with income level, at least in the lower income ranges, occurs in the frequency of ownership of U.S. savings bonds. On the other hand, frequency of ownership of life insurance increases sharply to the $5,000 level, approximately, where it tends to level off as it approaches 100 per cent. In general the evidence on frequency of ownership obtained from the Survey of Consumer Finances is in harmony with that obtained from Wisconsin tax returns.

SIZE OF HOLDINGS

The median provides perhaps the best measure of size of holding for types of financial asset where the distribution may be expected to be more or less skewed. Of course, in computing the median holding of each asset type for each income group, only individuals holding some amount of one of the specified assets were taken into account; that is, the Wisconsin sample is limited to those tax returns (single ones, or joint or combined returns of husband and wife both reporting income) that evidenced ownership of financial assets. Chart 3, which shows the median amount of each of four types of financial asset for different income ranges, indicates that size of holding increases with income. The median amount of time deposits and related claims changes least with income, and the median amount of direct debt assets held shows only a slightly greater change. It is the amount of corporate stock held that changes most with level of income.

Because in Chart 3 the median amounts of holdings of each type of asset are plotted on a logarithmic scale against income, the variation in the rate of increase in size of investment as incomes increase is clearly evident. Insofar as it is appropriate to judge from cross-section analysis of the practices of many individuals what the behavior of a single individual would be, it appears that only a comparatively moderate increase in the amount of funds placed in time deposits and related claims or in direct debt assets would occur with an increase of income. When income rises into the highest range ($50,000 and over), the rate of accretion to time deposits and related claims becomes smaller, while the rate of accretion to direct debt assets (tax-exempt bonds for the most part) continues unabated. On the other hand, holdings of traded stock increase at a fairly constant rate up to the $50,000 income level, but at a perceptibly lower rate thereafter. The most marked change occurs in connection with untraded stock. Up to the $10,000 level there is little change in the amount of untraded stock held as in-

INCOME STATUS AND INVESTMENT
CHART 3
Median Size of Holdings of Specified Types of Financial Asset, 1949, for Income Groups of Wisconsin Individuals

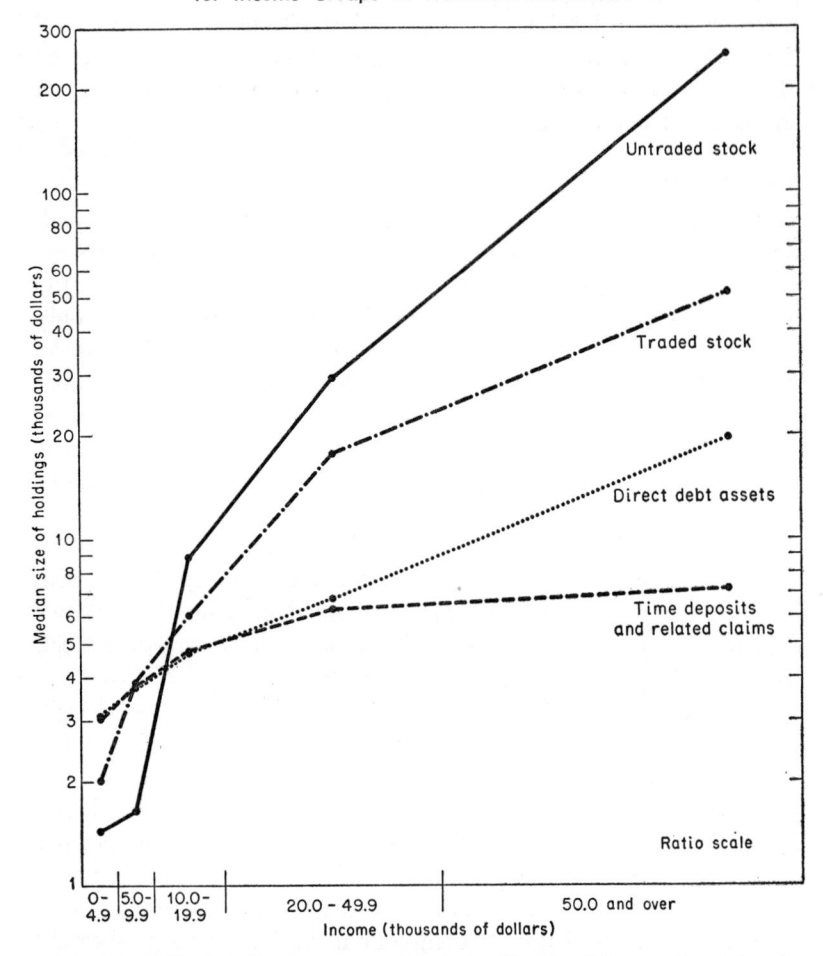

Based on Table A-6. Readings are centered at midpoints of income class intervals, except that for the $50,000 and over class the approximate mean, $90,000, is used.

come increases, but a substantial increase in amounts held occurs in the $10,000-to-$19,999 income range and continues, though at a somewhat diminished rate, throughout the remaining range of incomes.

Computation of the median amount of holdings of other types of asset for different income groups is difficult because the frequency distributions of the Survey of Consumer Finances contain an insufficient number of class intervals to permit accurate calculations. Nevertheless, Chart 4 shows estimates of median size of holding for three types of asset missing from the Wisconsin survey. If the calculations are correct, the median size of holdings of savings bonds and checking accounts shows little increase with income until somewhere past the $2,500 or $3,500 income mark. On the other hand, there seems to be a fairly steady increase in the size of life insurance holdings for successively higher income groups, at least judging from the median amount of premiums reported paid during 1950.

CHART 4

Estimated Median Size of Holdings of Specified Types of Financial Asset, for Income Groups of Spending Units in the United States

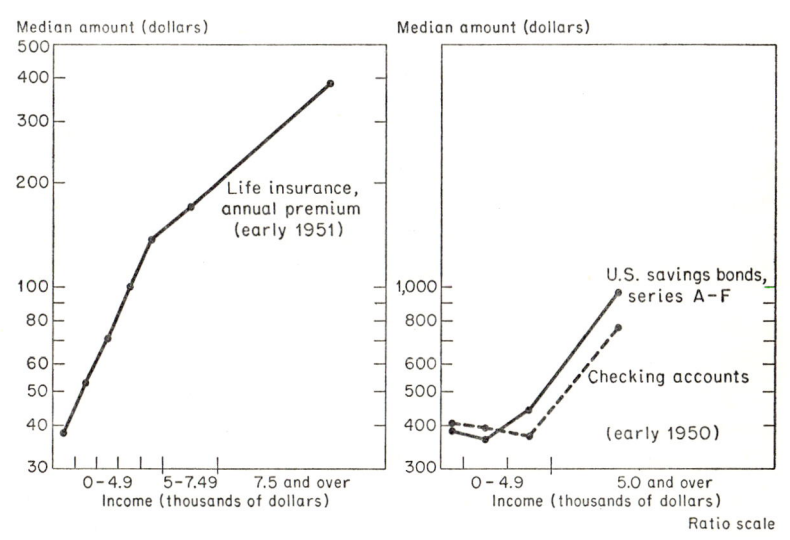

Computed from Survey of Consumer Finances data for checking accounts and United States savings bonds in Federal Reserve Bulletin, December 1950, Table 9, p. 1593, and for life insurance in the Bulletin of December 1951, Table 15, p. 1526.

Readings are centered at midpoints of income class intervals except that for open-end classes the approximate mean is used: $8,000 for owners of checking accounts and savings bonds with incomes of $5,000 and over; $12,500 for owners of life insurance with incomes of $7,500 and over.

The findings of the Wisconsin survey appear to be internally consistent in that for each type of asset both frequency of ownership and median size of holding increase with income in a fairly regular manner. On the other hand, the findings of the Survey of Consumer Finances concerning types of assets missing from the Wisconsin data lack that consistency. Whereas the frequency of ownership of life insurance does not increase much in ranges of income beyond the $5,000 level, the median size of holding does increase substantially with income. Similarly, frequency of ownership of savings bonds and checking accounts increases sharply with income in the lower income groups, but the average size of holding in the same range shows little change. These results, of course, may merely represent errors in calculating medians from insufficiently detailed frequency distributions or they may be true measures of types of assets differing, in their relationship to income, from those covered in the Wisconsin sample.

Comprehensive Measures of Financial Asset Ownership

The two attributes of asset ownership whose relation to personal income we have been examining—size of holding and frequency of ownership—combine to produce a pattern of dollar amounts of various types of asset that are held by different groups. This section will deal with the composition of financial asset holdings in particular ranges of income, relating differences in composition to differences in income level. In addition, it will contrast the several types of financial asset according to the manner in which they are distributed among different income groups.

COMPOSITION OF FINANCIAL
ASSET HOLDINGS

Table 8 shows the composition of financial asset holdings at various levels of income for the sample of Wisconsin individuals who reported receipt of interest or dividend income in 1949. Apart from the negative income group,[5] the higher the income group the larger the corporate equity component of total financial assets. Likewise, direct debt investment becomes more important as compared with time deposits and related claims. Even with demand deposits and federal government obligations missing from the account, debt assets—time deposits and related claims and direct debt—account for the major part of the financial assets held by individuals in the lower income group; only a small proportion of the holdings of the upper income groups are in debt form.

As one reads from low to higher income brackets, not only are

[5] The irregular behavior of the negative income group, whose data are supplied in the notes to this and subsequent tables, is undoubtedly the result of (1) the small number of sampled individuals coming within that category and (2) the peculiar and transitory nature of their incomes.

TABLE 8
Composition of Financial Asset Holdings for Income Groups of Wisconsin Individuals, 1949

Income	Time Deposits & Related Claims	Direct Debt Assets	Corporate Equity Assets	Total
$0-4,999	46.9%	22.9%	30.2%	100.0%
5,000-9,999	26.2	20.1	53.7	100.0
10,000-19,999	11.3	16.6	72.1	100.0
20,000-49,999	5.1	10.0	84.9	100.0
50,000 and over	1.2	5.5	93.3	100.0
All income groups[a]	24.5%	17.0%	58.5%	100.0%

Computed from Table A-3.

[a] Includes, besides the specified income groups, the small group reporting negative income, for whom the distribution (in the same order as above) was: 5.3%, 14.4%, 80.3%.

there substantial changes in the major types of assets held but definite trends are apparent within the major asset types themselves. Tables 9, 10, and 11 are constructed to show these variations. For successively higher income groups the major change in the category of time deposits and related claims is the tendency for individuals in the $5,000-to-$19,999 income groups to favor shares in savings and loan associations over similar investments carrying a lower return.

More pronounced changes of composition occur within the category of direct debt investments. In the lowest income group the

TABLE 9
Composition of Holdings of Time Deposits and Related Claims for Income Groups of Wisconsin Individuals, 1949

Income	Commercial Bank Savings Accounts	Savings & Loan Assn. Shares	Mutual Savings Bank Deposits	Credit Union Shares	Postal Savings Deposits	Total
$0-4,999	75.0%	20.8%	0.6%	1.7%	1.9%	100.0%
5,000-9,999	65.8	30.4	0.5	2.5	0.7	100.0
10,000-19,999	63.6	34.4	0.5	1.0	0.5	100.0
20,000-49,999	78.2	19.8	1.0	[a]	1.0	100.0
50,000 and over	73.8	23.8	2.4	[a]	[a]	100.0
All income groups[b]	72.7%	23.5%	0.6%	1.7%	1.5%	100.0%

Computed from Table A-3.

[a] Less than 0.05%.

[b] Includes, besides the specified income groups, the small group reporting negative income, whose holdings were divided between commercial savings bank accounts (76.9%) and savings and loan association shares (23.1%).

INCOME STATUS AND INVESTMENT

TABLE 10

Composition of Direct Debt Asset Holdings
for Income Groups of Wisconsin Individuals, 1949

Income	Notes of Individuals	Notes of Business Firms	State and Local Bonds[a]	Corporate Bonds	Total
$0-4,999	74.9%	12.9%	1.5%	10.7%	100.0%
5,000-9,999	55.8	25.4	3.0	15.9	100.0
10,000-19,999	50.9	27.7	3.8	17.6	100.0
20,000-49,999	34.1	35.1	12.0	18.8	100.0
50,000 and over	26.3	20.7	41.4	11.6	100.0
All income groups[b]	61.5%	19.7%	4.9%	13.9%	100.0%

Computed from Table A-3.
[a] Includes state, county, and municipal tax-exempt bonds.
[b] Includes, besides the specified income groups, the small group reporting negative income, for whom the distribution (in the same order as above) was: 61.9%, 6.7%, 3.8%, 27.6%.

TABLE 11

Composition of Corporate Equity Asset Holdings
for Income Groups of Wisconsin Individuals, 1949

Income	Traded Stock[a]	Untraded Stock[b]	Total
$0-4,999	77.2%	22.8%	100.0%
5,000-9,999	67.0	33.0	100.0
10,000-19,999	62.4	37.6	100.0
20,000-49,999	54.3	45.7	100.0
50,000 and over	43.1	56.9	100.0
All income groups[c]	60.5%	39.5%	100.0%

Computed from Table A-3.
[a] Based on market value.
[b] Based on market value equivalent.
[c] Includes, besides the specified income groups, the small group reporting negative income, for whom the distribution was: 78.9%, 21.1%.

notes of individuals and business firms are of overwhelming importance; in the high groups there is a pronounced shift to corporate bonds and to obligations of state, county, and municipal authorities. The predominance of the notes of individuals among direct debt investments, particularly in the low income group, deserves some comment. From an inspection of the original data it would appear that in the low income group the majority of such debt claims arose from real estate transactions; in the higher income groups, on the other hand, there is some evidence of a tendency for loans to be made between members of the same family, perhaps for security transactions. In the above-average income group one occasionally finds an individual who apparently was in the small loan business, but the net weight of such cases in the total is probably small. Many of the notes of business firms had been taken by the principal stockholder of a small corporation from its own firm. The reason for the relatively heavy holdings of state, county, and municipal bonds in the higher income groups is, of course, the tax advantage given to income from that source.[6]

The definite shift within corporate equity assets from traded to untraded stocks revealed in Table 11 for successively higher income groups, is difficult to interpret. While it may indicate a propensity, increasing with income, to hold riskier assets, there are doubts as to the validity of that interpretation. Despite the greater cost and time that may be involved in disposing of untraded stocks, there is no a priori reason to believe that as a group they are riskier than traded stocks. Furthermore, a substantial proportion of the amount of untraded stock held was owned by officers or major executives of the issuing corporations; indeed, many individuals were found in the higher income groups undoubtedly because they owned such business interest stock.[7] Perhaps the most reasonable interpretation is that heavy ownership of untraded stocks—amounting to the possession of controlling interest in a business—is a basis of higher income status rather than that these holdings manifest investor preferences among high income individuals.

What about the composition of asset holdings if all major types of income-earning assets are included in the calculation and also assets held primarily for liquidity purposes, such as cash and deposits? As part of a broad study of the effects of taxation upon different segments of the economy, a group under the auspices of the Graduate School of Business Administration of Harvard University has recently published statistics on asset composition for a sample of "active investors." The sample consists of 746 individuals chosen from the contact files of investment firms and is heavily concentrated in the upper income groups. Although the sample is hardly representative of the population at large, it is interesting to contrast the effects of income upon asset composition shown by the Harvard sample with those shown by the

---

[6] Despite the fact that individuals in the low income groups derive little benefit from the tax exemption feature of state and local government obligations, their holdings are considerable. See *The Ownership of Tax-Exempt Securities, 1913-1953*, by George E. Lent (National Bureau of Economic Research, Occasional Paper 47, 1955).

[7] See pages 96-98.

sample of Wisconsin investors. Because the Harvard study was not confined to the financial assets covered in the survey of Wisconsin investors, but includes such assets as interest in unincorporated businesses, rental property, cash value of insurance and annuities, and so on, its data provide insight into areas of personal investment missed by the Wisconsin survey.

Table 12 shows asset composition in 1949 for the Harvard

TABLE 12

Composition of Asset Holdings for Harvard Sample of Individual Investors Grouped by Income, 1949

TYPE OF ASSET	Under $7,500	$7,500- 12,499	$12,500- 24,999	$25,000- 49,999	$50,000- 99,999	$100,000 and Over
Cash, deposits, and U.S. government bonds	18%	21%	19%	13%	10%	14%
State and local securities	a	1	2	2	4	7
Senior corporate securities	8	6	3	4	3	5
Marketable common stock	40	34	28	27	19	28
Own business unincorporated	2	3	10	16	34	12
Own business incorporated	7	7	7	6	9	10
Other closely held corporations	1	2	6	6	7	6
Cash surrender value of insurance and annuities	6	9	9	7	4	3
Income-producing real estate	8	9	8	11	7	3
Notes and mortgages	1	a	1	2	2	a
Trusts[b]	6	5	6	6	1	12
Other	3	3	1	a	a	a
Total	100%	100%	100%	100%	100%	100%
Number of cases	193	173	156	120	42	24

From *Effects of Taxation: Investments by Individuals*, by J. Keith Butters, Lawrence E Thompson, and Lynn L. Bollinger (Harvard University, 1953), Table A-13, p. 468. Excludes 3 respondents whose size of income was not known.

a Less than 0.5%.

b Trusts include only trust property not managed or controlled by the respondent or a member of his immediate family unit.

sample of active investors. The following broad generalizations seem to be evident from the data:

1. By successively higher income groups a declining proportion of total assets is kept in the form of:
   a. Cash, deposits, and U.S. government bonds
   b. Senior corporate securities (bonds and preferred stocks)
   c. Marketable common stock
   d. Insurance and annuities
2. By successively higher income groups an increasing proportion of total assets is kept in the form of:
   a. State and local securities
   b. Owned unincorporated business
   c. Owned corporate business
   d. Other closely held stocks

Comparisons of asset composition at different income levels as revealed by the Harvard and the Wisconsin sample are made difficult by differences both in their respective classifications of assets and in the class intervals of their income distributions. The Harvard data apparently show that corporate stocks as a group (marketable and closely held, combined) were a declining proportion of total assets for successively higher income groups, although the decline is interrupted in the topmost income class. This is the major point of disagreement in the two sets of data. It is undoubtedly attributable to the fact that the Harvard sample probably was drawn from a universe "more venturesome than the general population within the income (and presumably also the wealth) groups covered by the active investor sample, especially in the lower and middle income (and wealth) ranges covered."[8] As the Harvard report suggests, part of the reason for the bias of the sample toward the more venturesome investors is the relatively heavy weight of individuals residing in major metropolitan areas rather than in medium-sized and small cities or rural areas. The geographic bias may also account for the smaller importance of closely held stock in the asset holdings of the individuals in the Harvard than in the Wisconsin sample.[9]

It is interesting to note that although data from the Harvard sample do not confirm the conclusion that equity investment in the form of corporate stock increases with income, yet they do indicate that if equity investment is redefined to include interest in unincorporated businesses and rental property as well as corporate

[8] J. Keith Butters, Lawrence E. Thompson, and Lynn L. Bollinger, *Effects of Taxation: Investments by Individuals* (Harvard University, 1953), p. 469.
[9] See pages 100-102.

stocks, the equity proportion of total asset holdings increases substantially for successively higher income groups up to the very highest, where the proportion decreases. In view of this evidence and the nature of the biases in the Harvard sample, it is believed that the conclusion based upon the Wisconsin material is not disproved.

THE DISTRIBUTION OF
FINANCIAL ASSETS

For much the same reason that the accuracy of frequency-of-ownership estimates derived from tax returns is dubious, estimates of the distribution of the dollar value of holdings of particular types of asset among income groups are suspect. It was evident in Chapter 3 that interest and dividend income reported on tax returns fell short of what might have been expected, and that therefore some proportion of the total value of each type of asset is missing from the survey estimates. Under these circumstances it is only proper to indicate that the distributions about to be presented assume that the missing amount of each type of asset is distributed in exactly the same manner as the known quantity.[10] Because of the inaccuracies probably resulting from that assumption, statements on the distribution of the dollar value of various types of asset among income groups will be couched in general terms only.

From Chart 5 it appears that in 1949 over half of the value of time deposits and related claims and about half of direct debt assets, but less than one-third of the total value of corporate stocks whether traded or untraded, were held by individuals with less than $5,000 income. Table 13 shows the estimated distribution of major types of financial assets missing from the Wisconsin data. Apparently from about one-half to two-thirds of the total value of checking accounts, of U.S. savings bonds, and of life insurance in 1950 was owned by individuals with incomes under $5,000.

What can be said about the concentration of ownership of different types of asset according to income level in view of the known biases inherent in the data?

A comparison of the concentrations of debt and equity assets is made difficult by the likelihood of different degrees of underreporting in different income groups, discussed in Chapter 3. If underreporting could be eliminated, probably the contrast in the patterns of concentration for debt and equity assets would, if any-

[10] See pages 54 f.

INCOME STATUS AND INVESTMENT

CHART 5

Income Distribution of the Population and of Specified Types of Financial Asset Holdings of Wisconsin Individuals, 1949

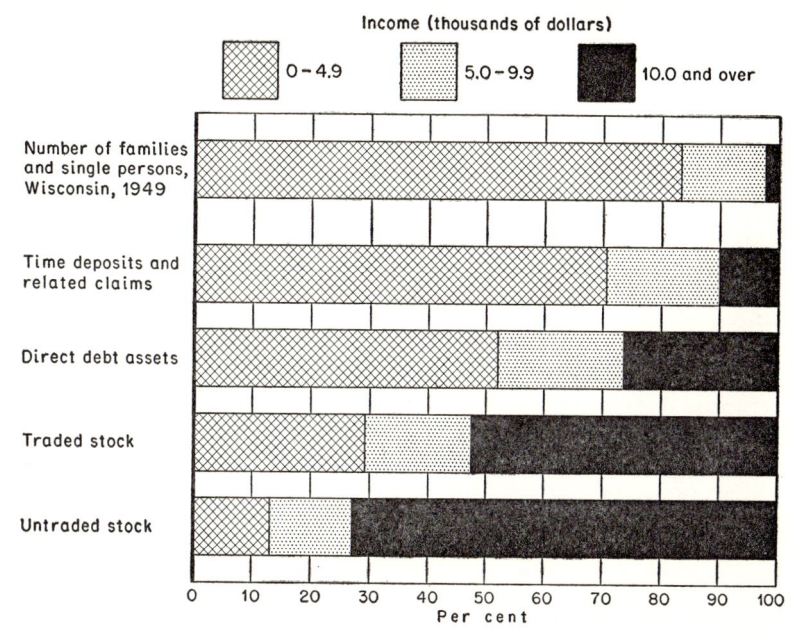

Based on estimates of holdings given in Table A-3. Population data from Census of Population: 1950, Vol. 2, Part 49, Wisconsin, Chapter B, Table 32, p. 49.

thing, be somewhat greater than that shown by the tax returns. Since the percentage of receipts unreported at the lower income levels appears to be greater for interest than for dividends, a correction for underreporting would increase the estimated debt assets of the lower income groups more than their stockholdings; but the effects on the holdings of either debt assets or corporate stocks in the higher income groups, where the percentage of unreported receipts is smaller, would probably be negligible.

One question of perpetual interest concerns the concentration of ownership of traded stocks as distinguished from equities of closely held corporations. Here the Wisconsin results differ rather substantially from results obtained through other recent surveys. Table 14 shows distributions of traded or marketable corporate stock based on the Wisconsin and the Harvard sample for 1949 and as estimated from the Survey of Consumer Finances for 1952. For the sake of comparison the boundary between low and middle income groups is set at $10,000 rather than $5,000. The volume

TABLE 13
Estimated Distributions of Value of Checking Accounts, U.S. Savings Bonds, and Life Insurance Premium Payments in the United States, 1950, by Income Group

INCOME	CHECKING ACCOUNTS[a] A	B	U.S. SAVINGS BONDS (SERIES A TO F)[a] A	B	LIFE INSURANCE PREMIUM PAYMENTS[b]
$0-1,000	4%	6%	3%	5%	3%
1,000-2,999	20	25	18	26	16
3,000-4,999	24	26	27	33	30
5,000 and over	53	43	52	36	51
Total	100%	100%	100%	100%	100%

[a] As of early 1950. The valuation data underlying the percentage distributions were estimated by first determining the number of spending units owning a specified type of asset in each size of holding class within income group, from percentage distributions given by the 1950 Survey of Consumer Finances (*Federal Reserve Bulletin*, June 1950, Table 4, p. 650, and December 1950, Table 9, p. 1593), and then multiplying the number of units in a group by an estimated typical value of holding for the group. In method A the median sizes of holding for income groups were calculated from the distribution of spending units by size of holding within income group, and then the medians were converted to assumed mean values by adjustment according to the curve of mean-median relationships found for holdings of time deposits and related claims by Wisconsin individuals (Table A-7). In method B the typical value used was the midpoint for each size-of-holding class, an assumed midpoint of $4,000 being chosen for the highest class ($2,000 and over).

[b] Represents the distribution of premiums only and therefore assumes a distribution of the cash surrender value of life insurance identical with the distribution of premium payments. Valuation figures were obtained by multiplying the average premium payments during 1950 for a given income group (as shown in *Life Insurance Fact Book, 1952*, Institute of Life Insurance, p. 14) by the estimated number of insured spending units in that income group in early 1951 (computed from data in "1951 Survey of Consumer Finances," *Federal Reserve Bulletin*, August 1951, Table 1, p. 921, and December 1951, Table 15, p. 1526).

of ownership in the income group below $10,000 as discovered by the Survey of Consumer Finances is the lowest, and that shown by the Wisconsin sample the highest, actually nearly half. It is conceivable that differences in the characteristics of the population in Wisconsin and the rest of the nation might be important in explaining some of the difference. For example, if Wisconsin stockholdings were more heavily concentrated in closely held corporations, as appears to be the case, we might expect to find fewer traded stocks in the higher income groups, where the closely held stocks tend to be concentrated.

In concluding the discussion of the distribution of financial asset ownership among income groups it seems worth while to re-emphasize basic skepticism as to the accuracy of survey findings showing,

INCOME STATUS AND INVESTMENT

TABLE 14

Estimated Distribution of the Value of
Traded or Marketable Stocks by Income Group:
Three Surveys Compared

INCOME OF HOLDER	WISCONSIN SAMPLE[a] (1949)	HARVARD STUDY[b] (1949) A	B	SURVEY OF CONSUMER FINANCES[c] (1952)
Under $10,000	48%	30%	25%	20%
10,000-49,999	36	37	39	80
50,000 and over	16	33	36	
Total	100%	100%	100%	100%

[a] Computed from Table A-3.
[b] From *Effects of Taxation: Investments by Individuals*, by J. Keith Butters, Lawrence E. Thompson, and Lynn L. Bollinger (Harvard University, 1953), Table XVII-7, p. 438. The authors consider estimate A as a minimum estimate for concentration of marketable stock holdings in the income range of $10,000 and over, and estimate B as the more probable.
[c] From "Stock Ownership among American Families," by George Katona, John B. Lansing, and Peter E. deJanosi, *Michigan Business Review*, January 1953, p. 16.

for instance, that X per cent of a particular type of financial asset is held by individuals with incomes under $5,000 or is held by the group receiving $10,000 and over. Until data-collecting methods are improved to the point that survey results account for a greater proportion of the total amount known to be outstanding, we can never be sure that the amount of assets unaccounted for by a particular survey is uniformly or proportionately distributed among the several income groups rather than concentrated in a particular one. The present findings, therefore, are offered as merely indicative of the ranks of concentration of particular types of asset in stated income groups. Summarizing, it is found that the ranking of the various types of financial asset according to the proportion held by individuals with less than $5,000 income is as follows:

Rank	Type of Asset
1	Time deposits and related claims
2	Direct debt assets / Checking accounts, savings bonds, and life insurance
3	Traded stock
4	Untraded stock

INCOME STATUS AND INVESTMENT

CAUSE AND EFFECT

So far in the analysis the implication has been that the income level of the individual determines the pattern of financial assets owned by him. Surely there is much to that view. A person of low or moderate income undoubtedly has a greater need for liquidity than a person of high income, merely because of the difficulty (time, sacrifice, etc.) involved in raising a given sum from either income or resources. Somewhat the same relationship may exist between market risk and income—a subject to be taken up in another chapter. Yet while the line of causation from income to type of asset held is undoubtedly of prime importance, there are other lines of causation which bear looking into.

Clearly, the relation between income and the pattern of financial asset ownership is not one-way. Total income is in part determined by investment income, and investment income in turn is determined by the composition of financial assets. In the Wisconsin sample, interest and dividends together amounted to only 4 per cent of total income for reporting taxpayers in the lowest income group, but to 39 per cent in the highest income group (Table 15). The presence of income-earning financial assets, therefore, is important

TABLE 15
Relative Importance of Reported Components of Income for Income Groups of Wisconsin Individuals Having Financial Assets, 1949

TYPE OF INCOME	$0-4.9	$5.0-9.9	$10.0-19.9	$20.0-49.9	$50.0 & Over	TOTAL
Wages and salaries	95.2%	86.5%	52.5%	52.5%	37.1%	75.4%
Interest	1.7	1.4	2.2	1.8	1.5	1.7
Dividends	2.2	2.9	10.3	16.9	37.2	11.7
Rent	0.1	0.7	2.0	1.7	0.9	0.6
Capital gains (or loss)	0.1	1.7	4.6	3.6	9.3	2.8
Business profits	0.6	5.3	20.9	12.3	4.8	4.2
Trust income	a	0.2	0.8	1.6	2.2	0.7
Partnership income	0.1	1.3	6.7	9.6	7.0	2.9
Total	100.0%	100.0%	100.0%	100.0%	100.0%	100.0%

Distributions are from survey estimates based on the sum of the income components reported on sampled tax returns. The sum of the reported income components differs from the total income reported on the tax forms by an amount representing the net difference between income from sources other than those indicated above and deductions of business expenses and nontaxable income previously reported under one of the identified components. This difference is relatively small, accounting for less than 5% of total reported income in each income class.

a Less than 0.05%.

in determining the general shape of the distribution of income. Although to eliminate the income yielded by financial assets would not disturb the ranking of the Wisconsin sample so long as income groups as a whole were considered, undoubtedly the individuals in the sample would be drastically reranked if each individual's noninterest and nondividend income only were considered.

Even more directly, the pattern of financial asset ownership affects income status. It has been observed that for the higher income groups a greater proportion of the amount of asset holdings is in high-paying corporate equities than for the low income groups, who tend to favor direct debt and deposit types of claims, assets which in good times tend to be less remunerative than corporate stocks. What does that phenomenon mean in terms of differences in investment income received by the various income groups? Table 16 indicates that the yield received by the topmost income group ($50,000 and over) is more than half again higher than the yield received on all financial assets held by the lowest income group (under $5,000), merely because of the greater proportion of high-income-earning assets in the former group. The measure used, the hypothetical yield in Table 16, considers only group averages for the three major types of assets and does not consider that part of the yield differences among income groups attributable to the superior selection of particular assets in any one general

TABLE 16

Actual and Hypothetical Yields from Financial Asset Holdings of Wisconsin Individuals Grouped by Income, 1949

Income	Actual Yield[a]	Hypothetical Yield[b]
$0-4,999	3.71%	3.70%
5,000-9,999	4.60	4.80
10,000-19,999	5.47	5.62
20,000-49,999	5.98	6.04
50,000 and over	6.79	6.32
All income groups[c]	4.94%	4.94%

[a] Computed from Tables A-1 and A-3.
[b] Calculated from actual yields on the major types of asset for all income groups combined—1.37% for time deposits and related claims, 4.81% for direct debt assets, and 6.47% for corporate equity assets—by weighting the yields according to the composition of a given income group's total holdings, Table 8.
[c] Includes, besides the specified income groups, the small group reporting negative income, for whom the yields were: 5.85%, 5.96%.

asset group. It is quite clear that differences in return on investments for broad groups of individuals shown in the table were, in 1949, due less to the canny selection of particular stocks by persons in the higher income groups than to their ability, willingness, or desire to hold a comparatively large proportion of assets in corporate issues of capital stock.

There remains the possibility that it is the total wealth status of the individual which is most important in determining the pattern of financial asset holdings and that the strong association between income and wealth produces a spurious correlation between income and the pattern of financial asset ownership. Table 17 shows the composition of asset holdings of the Harvard sample of active investors. Actually, while trust holdings, unincorporated businesses, and state and local securities tend to increase in importance with wealth, marketable common stock declines in importance, as do life insurance and the group including cash, deposits, and federal bonds. Even from this tabulation we do not know whether it is wealth or income which determines the pattern of financial asset holdings.

The best evidence on that question is from the Wisconsin sample and is shown in Chart 6, which is a study of the proportionate holdings of each type of financial asset simultaneously by income and by a rough measure of wealth, the amount of financial assets held. It appears that both income and wealth are important causative factors in determining the composition of an individual's financial assets. Within each income group, as individuals with larger financial asset holdings are considered, an increasing proportion of the amount held is found to consist of corporate equities.[11] Furthermore, within each size class of financial asset holdings corporate equities become more important the higher the income group. In the lower income group, as individuals with more assets are considered, the proportion of funds held in the form of direct debt investment is found to increase. That this is not true in the higher income groups is probably because corporate bond yields compare unfavorably with stock yields and because there is less need in the high income groups for safety of investment.

The finding that both income and wealth seem to be related to

[11] The use of book value to measure untraded stock holdings in Chart 16 (rather than the market value equivalent used elsewhere in the chapter) imparts some upward bias to the tendency for corporate equity holdings to increase with income and with size of asset holdings, but it probably does not affect the conclusion.

TABLE 17
Composition of Asset Holdings for Harvard Sample of Individual Investors Grouped by Wealth, 1949

TYPE OF ASSET	Under $25,000	$25,000-49,999	$50,000-99,999	WEALTH OF INVESTOR $100,000-249,999	$250,000-499,999	$500,000-999,999	$1,000,000 and Over
Cash, deposits, and U.S. government bonds	35%	23%	23%	17%	15%	15%	10%
State and local securities	a	a	1	1	2	3	5
Senior corporate securities	3	5	5	5	4	4	4
Marketable common stock	36	39	35	31	27	30	21
Own business unincorporated	a	1	3	8	16	12	22
Own business incorporated	6	5	9	9	6	9	8
Other closely held corporations	1	2	3	4	6	5	7
Cash surrender value of insurance and annuities	15	13	11	9	6	6	2
Income-producing real estate	3	10	7	8	11	6	6
Notes and mortgages	1	a	a	a	1	a	1
Trusts[b]	a	2	2	6	5	9	14
Other	a	a	1	2	1	1	a
Total	100%	100%	100%	100%	100%	100%	100%
Number of cases	146	120	130	156	76	40	41

From *Effects of Taxation: Investments by Individuals*, by J. Keith Butters, Lawrence E. Thompson, and Lynn L. Bollinger (Harvard University, 1953), Table A-13, p. 468. Excludes 37 respondents whose wealth status was not known.
[a] Less than 0.5%.
[b] Trusts include only trust property not managed or controlled by the respondent or a member of his immediate family unit.

INCOME STATUS AND INVESTMENT

CHART 6

Composition of Financial Asset Holdings for Wisconsin Individuals Grouped by Size of Holdings within Income Group, 1949

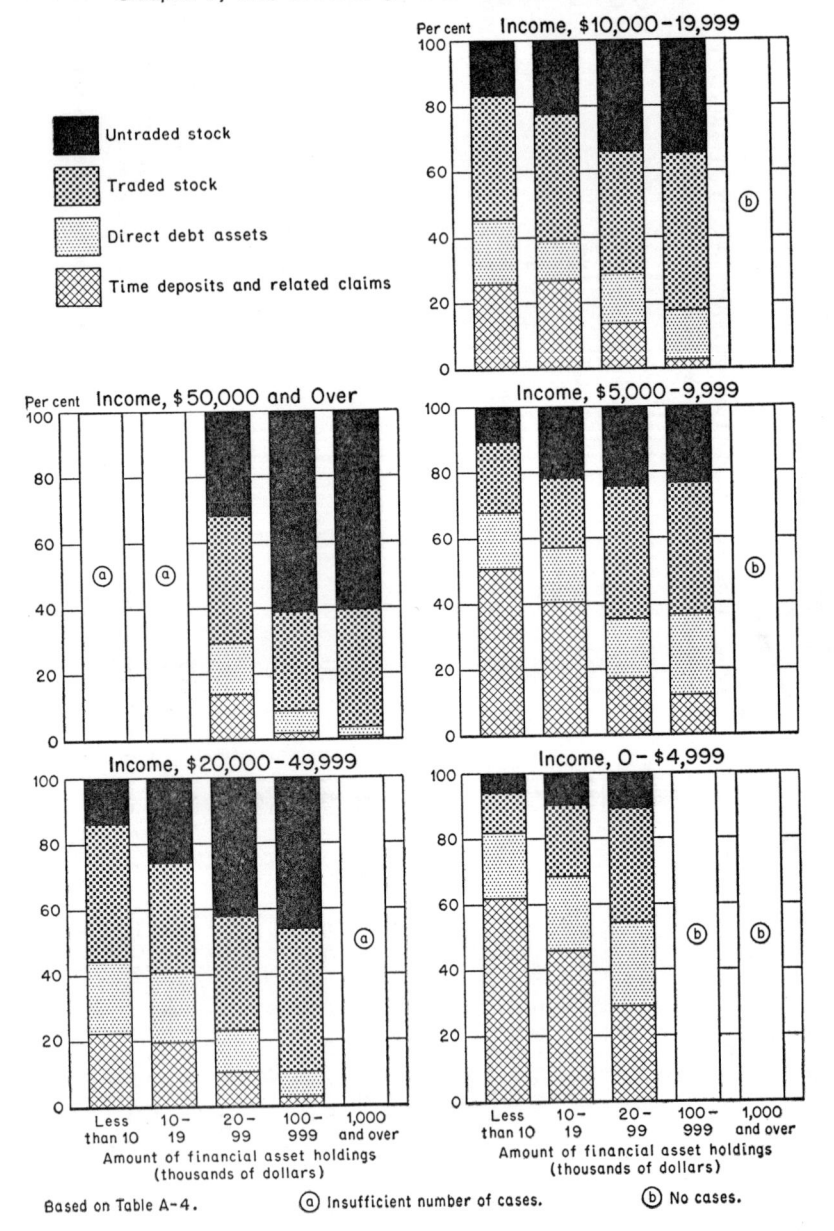

Legend:
- Untraded stock
- Traded stock
- Direct debt assets
- Time deposits and related claims

Panels: Income, $10,000–19,999; Income, $50,000 and Over; Income, $5,000–9,999; Income, $20,000–49,999; Income, 0–$4,999

Horizontal axis (per panel): Amount of financial asset holdings (thousands of dollars) — Less than 10, 10–19, 20–99, 100–999, 1,000 and over

Based on Table A-4.   (a) Insufficient number of cases.   (b) No cases.

the pattern of financial assets raises the question of which factor may be the more closely associated with asset composition. In the lower ranges of income and asset size, where the relationships (for the Wisconsin sample) are approximately linear, the proportion of the value of financial assets consisting of corporate equities seems to vary more with income than with the size of asset holdings. A doubling of income from $5,000 to $10,000, with asset size held constant, is accompanied by an increase of 10 percentage points in the proportionate amount of equity holdings, while a doubling of the amount of financial assets from $5,000 to $10,000, with income held constant, is accompanied by a rise of only about 6 percentage points. In the upper ranges of income and asset holdings the opposite appears to be the case. A doubling of income from $20,000 to $40,000 is accompanied by a rise of only about 2 percentage points in the proportionate amount of corporate equity assets, while a similar doubling of asset holdings, income held constant, is accompanied, as before, by a rise of about 6 percentage points in equities. One possible factor bearing on this problem comes in the next chapter, where we shall observe that particularly in the case of closely held issues, stock owners are frequently major executives of the corporation. Examination of the individual income tax returns left the very distinct impression that in some cases the ownership of stock in the corporation was a major qualification required of individuals drawing large executive salaries from small and medium-sized corporations. The ownership of particular financial assets, in other words, partially determines the size of wage and salary income. In the case of these so-called business interest holdings, therefore, there is good reason to believe that the character and size of investment assets may well play a causative role not only in determining that component of income derived directly from the investment but also in determining salary income through the exercise of prerogatives of control.

In addition there is the possibility, of course, that the unique character and abilities of certain individuals might lead them not only to occupations and particular situations more remunerative than the average, but also to choices of more remunerative types of investments. Such an explanation, presuming both a rather absolute form of economic motivation and the absence of restrictions upon accomplishing the desired results, would regard both income status and investment practices as subject to causation from variables in human personality and training.

INCOME STATUS AND INVESTMENT

The fairly obvious conclusion to be drawn from the foregoing discussion is that the lines of cause and effect running between investment practices of individuals and their economic status are exceedingly complex. At least in the lower income levels, the association of investment patterns and income is stronger than the association between investment patterns and the rather inadequate measure of wealth status afforded by the data. On the other hand, the amount and composition of asset holdings certainly affect income directly through investment earnings and occasionally affect the ability to earn labor rewards. Personality factors, including training, also may influence both income and type and size of investment holdings. In spite of the reasons to believe that income is not necessarily the determining variable in all cases, the evidence of positive association between income and investment composition is too consistent and the logic too convincing to be entirely refuted.

The principal findings of this chapter are:

1. For each type of financial asset, both the frequency of ownership and the median size of holding tend to increase for successively higher income groups.

2. There is a significant shift in the composition of financial asset holdings as measured by dollar value for successively higher income groups of the population. If only the financial assets covered in tax returns are considered, ownership shifts from predominantly debt assets of time deposit or direct type in the lowest income group to corporate equities in the higher income groups. In general, the trend toward increased equity ownership for higher income groups is apparent even if the analysis includes demand deposits, U.S. savings bonds, life insurance, ownership of unincorporated businesses, etc.

3. The various types of financial asset differ widely in their distribution among the income strata of the population. In general, the major holders of deposits, of life insurance, and of direct debt, including savings bonds, seem to be the lower income groups, while the higher income groups appear to be the major holders of corporate stocks.

4. Cause-and-effect relationships between the income level of the individual and the types of assets in which he chooses to invest funds are complex. The favored explanation is, of course, that income levels determine basic attitudes toward risk and liquidity and therefore the broad outlines of investment policy. However, investment policy in turn affects income, not only through direct

yields from investments but also because substantial holdings of stock in a corporation, especially if they constitute a controlling interest, may enhance the investor's opportunity to receive executive salaries.

CHAPTER 5

The Effects of Occupation and City Size on Investment in Financial Assets

AMONG factors other than income which have a systematic effect upon the distribution of financial asset ownership and which play a part in determining what types of financial assets are held by particular individuals, both the occupation of the individual involved and the size of city in which he resides appear significant. For example, about one-third of the reason why individuals with incomes of $10,000 and over, as a group, hold a greater proportion of their financial assets in traded stock than the group with less than $5,000 income appears to be the concentration in the higher income group of certain occupations that seem naturally to involve large holdings of traded stock. Partly the analysis of occupation and city size supplements the study of the relation between income and financial investment behavior; in the language of correlation analysis, the correlation is improved by the addition of these variables. But analysis of them also adds new dimensions to the study, each of which is of interest and importance in itself.

In general, the investor's occupation and the size of the city in which he resides apparently influence financial investment patterns in such a manner that it is impracticable to treat them as continuous variables having a direct effect upon financial behavior. Systems of classifying persons according to occupation are not stated in terms of continuous variables, and the effect of occupation on individual investment practices appears to operate more through the form (and financing requirements) of business associated with different occupations than through the occupational factor itself. Similarly, although size classifications of communities may be stated as continuous variables, the effect of city size on the practices of investors appears to be less that of population density directly than that of differences in the characteristics of business organization in communities of different sizes. The latter factor in turn reflects variations in resource distribution of which the distribution of the population is but one part. Thus the classification of individuals by size of city of residence is less an attempt to relate population density to investment behavior than to use the factor of city size as a substitute for a whole set of less measurable influences.

There appears to be some degree of correlation among the income level of an individual, his occupation, and the size of the city in which he lives. The income level of professional and managerial persons is, of course, higher, and that of unskilled labor lower, than the average for all earners, and these differences are also noticeable in total family income. Similarly, persons and families living in rural areas and small communities have lower incomes than do those residing in metropolitan areas. To some extent community size differences in income are a product of the occupational "mix" of the community, although they are evident even within certain occupations. Because of the correlation between income level and these other factors, the analysis attempts to isolate the effect of income on asset composition and to consider separately the effect of occupation and city size. It was not practical, however, to remove the interaction between occupation and city size, because the detailed subclassification required for such an analysis might have produced too few cases in many of the cells, so that the statistical reliability of observed differences would have been doubtful.

The examination of such additional factors and their influence on the investment practices of individuals is necessarily incomplete. Many other factors affecting investment preference patterns undoubtedly exist—such as age, sex, education, and dependency status—that may have a greater or lesser importance than occupation and city size. But the attempts that were made to explore their effect on financial investment were not fruitful, partly because of difficulties involved in measuring the variables from information stated on tax returns and partly because the effects of some of them were apparently slight.

Occupation

All individuals in the Wisconsin sample were classified according to occupation as given on their tax returns. In the case of joint or combined returns of husband and wife both reporting income, if both were gainfully employed, the classification chosen was that of the husband, except in one or two cases where it was apparent that the husband had worked only intermittently during the year. In many cases the classification had to be quite arbitrary and the difference between some classifications, such as the skilled and semiskilled on the one hand, and unskilled labor on the other, was not at all precise. Persons stating their occupation as "laborer" were put in the unskilled category, as were those stating certain types of menial occupation (janitor, helper, "odd jobs," etc.). On the other hand, persons stating specific occupations such as "press operator" or "core maker" were placed in the skilled and semiskilled category, even though the degree of technical skill necessary in the particular job was unknown. In a few instances the occupational category appeared not to match the income reported in a particular situation; in some of these cases occupation was not taken as stated. A tendency for some persons to "write up" their occupations—bookkeepers, for example, listing themselves as accountants—was apparent.

The greatest difficulty encountered was in attempting to classify high income individuals on the basis of a relatively simple occupational scale designed, in the main, for low income individuals. Thus a $40,000-a-year "sales agent" was classified as "clerical and sales" even though his duties may have been largely executive or managerial. Some individuals in the sample listed themselves as "investor" or "capitalist"; these were placed in the catch-all group— "all others and unspecified." Although the catch-all group also contains students and unemployed persons, as well as persons not specifying their occupation, it is heavily weighted by the financial assets of persons specifying "investor" or "capitalist" as their occupation. Widows are included in the category of housewives, as are single women without occupation deriving their income mainly from property.

Country-wide data on the frequency of ownership of financial assets, derived from the 1949 Survey of Consumer Finances, show the proportion of spending units headed by persons with various occupations that hold different types of financial assets.[1] Summarized in Table 18, this material reveals that only about half of the units headed by unskilled laborers held one or more types of "liquid assets" (savings accounts, checking accounts, and federal bonds), whereas almost nine-tenths of the units headed by professional and managerial and self-employed persons held such assets. In the case of corporate stocks, 15 per cent of all units headed by persons in professional and managerial pursuits held

[1] For a definition of a spending unit, see Chapter 2, footnote 10. Some units consist of a single person, and the expression "headed by" is not intended to imply their exclusion.

EFFECTS OF OCCUPATION AND CITY SIZE

TABLE 18

Frequency of Ownership of Liquid Assets and of Corporate Stock for Occupational Groups of Spending Units in the United States, Early 1949

OCCUPATION	PERCENTAGE OF UNITS HOLDING:	
	Liquid Assets[a]	Corporate Stock[b]
Professional	91%	15%
Managerial and self-employed	88	15
Clerical and sales	84	9
Skilled and semiskilled	70	4
Unskilled	49	
Farm operator	72	14
Retired	70	9

From "1949 Survey of Consumer Finances," *Federal Reserve Bulletin*, August 1949, Table 5, p. 903, and *ibid.*, October 1949, Table 17, p. 1196.

[a] Includes checking accounts, savings accounts, and U.S. government bonds of all types.

[b] Includes common and preferred stocks of corporations open to investment by the general public.

issues of corporations open to public investment; in contrast, only 4 per cent of the units headed by skilled and unskilled laboring persons held any stocks of that type. Surprisingly, the Survey of Consumer Finances data show that farmers are nearly as frequent holders of corporate stocks as are spending units headed by professional and managerial persons.

Similar differences in the distribution of financial asset holdings among occupational groups are revealed by the Wisconsin tax returns. These can be observed in Chart 7, in which the dollar amount of each of the main types of assets held, and the number of holders of each, are distributed percentagewise among occupational groups. The results may be compared with the occupational distribution of all families and single persons in the United States. Thus, Wisconsin individuals in five occupational groups—professional, clerical and sales, skilled and semiskilled, unskilled labor and farm laborers, and farm operators—constituted about 68 per cent of the family population in 1949 and held about 67 per cent of the dollar value of time deposits and related claims, 38 per cent of the direct debt assets, 27 per cent of the value of traded stocks, and 16 per cent of the value of untraded stocks.

Eleven per cent of the family population consists of individuals in managerial and nonfarm self-employed pursuits. This numerically small group has greater importance among holders of financial

89

EFFECTS OF OCCUPATION AND CITY SIZE

CHART 7

Occupational Distribution of the Population, and of Financial Asset Ownership by Wisconsin Individuals in 1949

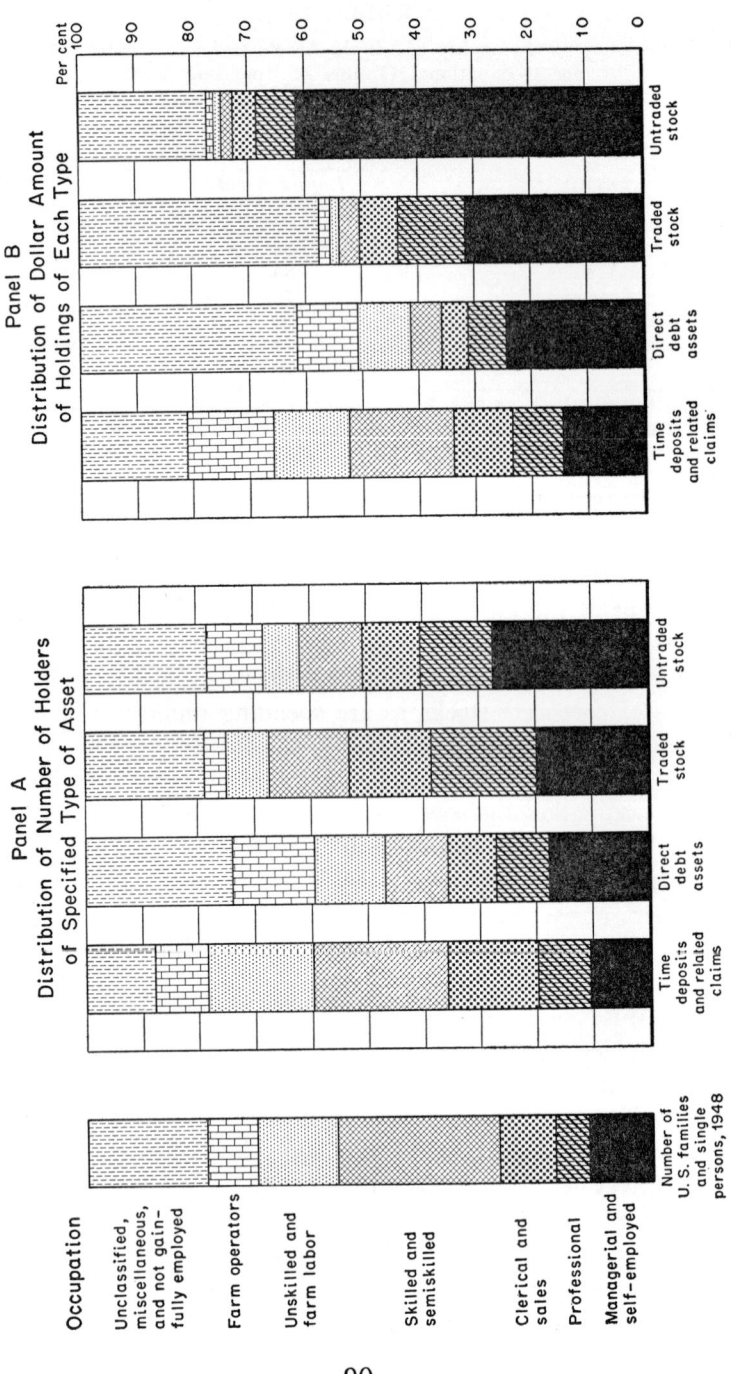

Panel A
Distribution of Number of Holders of Specified Type of Asset

Panel B
Distribution of Dollar Amount of Holdings of Each Type

Occupation:
- Unclassified, miscellaneous, and not gainfully employed
- Farm operators
- Unskilled and farm labor
- Skilled and semiskilled
- Clerical and sales
- Professional
- Managerial and self-employed

Panel A from Table A-7, Panel B from Table A-8, and occupational distribution for the United States from preliminary data in Current Population Reports of the Bureau of the Census.

assets than its proportion in the population would indicate. Sampled individuals in the managerial and self-employed group constituted 10 per cent of the number of holders of time deposits, 18 per cent of the total holders of debt instruments, 20 per cent of the holders of traded stocks, and 28 per cent of the holders of untraded stocks. Even greater concentration in this occupational group is indicated when the distribution of the dollar value of asset holdings is examined. Self-employed and managerial persons held, in terms of total dollar value, 14 per cent of the time deposits, 24 per cent of the debt instruments, 31 per cent of the traded stocks, and 61 per cent of the untraded stocks surveyed.

Finally, there is a group of individuals who are not normally in the labor force but who appear nonetheless as important holders of certain types of financial assets. It includes widows, housewives, retired persons, and "investors" or "capitalists" (i.e. persons living on property income), and some others. While the group holds only a moderate share of time deposits or untraded stocks, it holds approximately two-fifths of the total value of both debt instruments and traded stocks (38 and 42 per cent, respectively). It should be noted, however, that these figures probably overstate the importance of individuals not in the labor force because of the presence in the catch-all category—"unclassified, miscellaneous, and not gainfully employed"—of some persons who did not specify their occupations.

Table 19 shows estimates of the distribution of checking accounts, U.S. savings bonds, and life insurance among occupational groups in the United States for 1950, based on the 1950 and 1951 Surveys of Consumer Finances. It is quite apparent that the "all other" occupational group, including retired persons, holds as great a share of the value of checking accounts and savings bonds as of the nonequity types of asset covered by the Wisconsin survey, though its share of life insurance is smaller. On the other hand, spending units headed by managerial or self-employed persons stand out as large holders of all three of the types of asset not covered in the Wisconsin sample—checking accounts, savings bonds, and life insurance. Farmers, while making up 9 per cent of the population, hold about 16 per cent of the value of checking accounts, but only about 5 per cent of the life insurance. Skilled and semiskilled workers hold a share of life insurance about equal to their proportion in the population, but a smaller share of savings bonds and a still smaller share of checking accounts.

TABLE 19
Estimated Distributions of Value of Checking Accounts, U.S. Savings Bonds, and Life Insurance Premium Payments in the United States, 1950, by Occupational Group

OCCUPATION	CHECKING ACCOUNTS[a] A	B	U.S. SAVING BONDS, SERIES A TO F[a] A	B	LIFE INSURANCE PREMIUM PAYMENTS[b]
Professional and semiprofessional	10%	11%	13%	12%	12%
Managerial and self-employed	20	24	16	18	29
Clerical and sales	9	10	11	12	13
Skilled and semiskilled	10	10	16	16	26
Unskilled and service	3	3	4	5	4
Farm operator	16	16	6	9	5
All other (including retired)	33	26	34	28	10
Total	100%	100%	100%	100%	100%

[a] As of early 1950. The valuation data underlying the percentage distributions were estimated by first determining the number of spending units owning a specified type of asset in each size-of-holding class within occupational group, from percentage distributions given by the 1950 Survey of Consumer Finances (*Federal Reserve Bulletin*, July 1950, Table 11, p. 787, and December 1950, Table 34, p. 1607), and then multiplying the number of units in a group by an estimated typical value of holding for the group. In method A the median size of holding for a given occupational group was calculated from the distribution of spending units by size of holding within occupation, and was converted to an assumed mean value as follows: The curve of mean-median relationships for size of holdings of time deposits and similar claims by Wisconsin individuals was plotted by income class (Table A-6), and the relationship applicable to each occupational group was read off at the appropriate point on the income scale (mean income for the occupational group being available from the *Federal Reserve Bulletin*, August 1950, Table 2, p. 950, except that for the "all other" group an assumed figure, $1,500, had to be used); and the calculated median for the occupational group was adjusted accordingly. In method B the typical value used was the midpoint for each size-of-holding class, an assumed midpoint of $4,000 being chosen for the highest class ($2,000 and over).

[b] Represents the distribution of premiums only and therefore assumes a distribution of the cash surrender value of life insurance identical with the distribution of premium payments. Valuation figures were obtained by multiplying average premium payments during 1950 for a given occupational group (as shown in *Life Insurance Fact Book, 1952*, Institute of Life Insurance, p. 14) by the estimated number of insured spending units in that group in early 1951 (computed from data in "1951 Survey of Consumer Finances," *Federal Reserve Bulletin*, August 1951, Table 7, p. 927, and December 1951, Table 15, p. 1526).

The various occupational groups have been arranged in Chart 8 in ascending order of the proportion of their total financial assets consisting of corporate equities. The two groups of Wisconsin individuals with the smallest proportion of their holdings taking the form of corporate stocks—farm operators and unskilled labor—have practically identical asset composition. Both farm operators and unskilled laborers hold amounts of direct debt assets that are large in comparison with the proportions held by other occupational groups; in the first case this probably results from the customary methods of financing agriculture, in which sales of land

EFFECTS OF OCCUPATION AND CITY SIZE

CHART 8

Composition of Financial Asset Holdings for Occupational Groups of Wisconsin Individuals, 1949

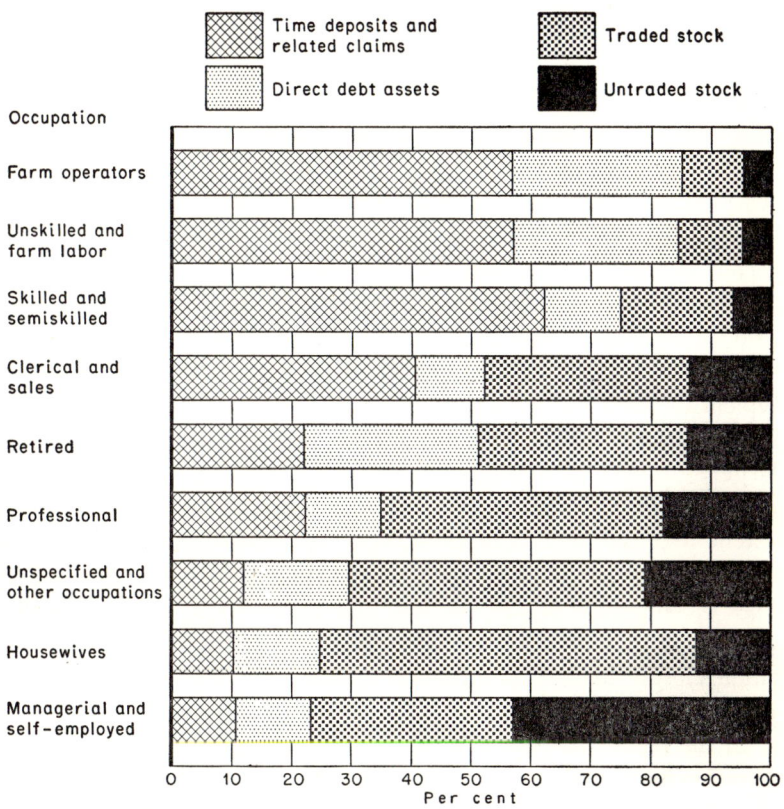

Based on Table A-8.

and livestock are frequently executed by the exchange of notes or mortgages rather than of cash. No similar explanation is available for the comparatively heavy holding of direct debt assets by unskilled laborers. Retired individuals, it will be noted, are also included among the relatively heavy holders of direct debt assets.

At the other extreme, housewives hold a greater proportion of their financial assets in the form of traded stock (nearly two-thirds of the dollar value of their holdings) than does any other group, while managerial and self-employed persons have the heaviest proportionate holdings of untraded stocks (43 per cent). It is not difficult to see the advantage of traded stocks for housewives—in

EFFECTS OF OCCUPATION AND CITY SIZE

the group surveyed, probably widows for the most part. Traded stocks have a high yield and are relatively liquid in case of emergency. The large holdings of untraded stocks by the managerial and self-employed group undoubtedly reflect investment in owned or controlled corporations, about which more will be said below.

Further light on the relation of occupational differences to the composition of financial asset holdings is given by Table 20, which divides each occupational group into three income classes so that occupational differences in asset composition may be viewed separately from the influence of income. It will be observed that the earlier generalization about the investment pattern followed by the managerial and self-employed does not hold for such of the group as have incomes of less than $5,000. These actually have a smaller share of their holdings in the form of corporate stocks than is typical for their income group as a whole. It may be that the lowest income group among the managerial and self-employed consists largely of owners of unincorporated businesses, while corporate executives predominate in the higher income groups. Thus, to the extent that the owners of unincorporated businesses plow back a considerable part of their savings into their businesses, their holdings of corporate stocks are low and exceeded by the ownership interest in their own unincorporated enterprises. Furthermore, the small closely held corporations whose owners were in the income category under $5,000 may have been non-dividend-paying firms, with the result that the estimate of untraded stocks held by managers in that income group is too low. It is also interesting to note that farm operators in the lowest income group do not have markedly larger holdings of direct debt assets than the average for their income group. The most likely reason for their difference in that respect from farmers in higher income groups is the fact that notes, mortgages, etc., originate largely through the sale of land and other physical assets, which only the wealthier farmers would have in any great abundance.[2]

[2] In Wisconsin the ownership of farms through mortgage financing has generally been preferred to tenancy and for that reason active and retired farmers there might be expected to hold a considerably greater proportion of their assets in the form of debt instruments than in states where high tenancy ratios prevail. See *Farm Management*, by John D. Black, Marion Clawson, Charles R. Sayre, and Walter W. Wilcox (New York, 1947), p. 708, and Chart 99, p. 709.

TABLE 20

Composition of Financial Asset Holdings of Wisconsin Individuals Grouped by Occupation within Income Group, 1949

Income Group and Type of Asset	Professional	Managerial and Self-employed	Clerical & Sales	Skilled & Semi-skilled	Unskilled	Farm Operators	House-wives, etc.	Retired	All Others & Unspecified	All Occupations
$0-4,999										
Time dep., etc.	38.7%	51.4%	55.4%	64.1%	59.1%	62.2%	18.7%	29.0%	27.5%	46.9%
Direct debt	12.6	24.9	11.3	14.3	25.2	25.3	19.2	35.8	27.5	23.0
Traded stock	39.1	12.7	24.1	18.0	11.1	8.9	55.9	25.4	36.9	23.3
Untraded stock	9.5	11.0	9.2	3.6	4.6	3.6	6.2	9.8	8.1	6.8
Total	100.0	100.0	100.0	100.0	100.0	100.0	100.0	100.0	100.0	100.0
$5,000-9,999										
Time dep., etc.	26.6	20.4	35.3	63.6	37.2	36.3	7.7	26.9	10.5	26.2
Direct debt	12.3	24.1	11.7	5.8	49.3	33.1	14.6	29.8	19.1	20.2
Traded stock	47.0	26.6	37.3	21.9	6.4	19.2	76.0	32.4	39.6	36.0
Untraded stock	14.1	28.9	15.7	8.7	7.1	11.4	1.7	10.9	30.8	17.5
Total	100.0	100.0	100.0	100.0	100.0	100.0	100.0	100.0	100.0	100.0
$10,000 and over										
Time dep., etc.	12.8	5.1	10.1	15.6	a	3.5	3.8	3.3	2.6	5.8
Direct debt	12.9	9.2	12.5	23.4	a	79.3	9.7	11.7	13.2	10.6
Traded stock	50.7	37.3	55.3	7.8	a	6.9	61.0	59.4	52.9	43.9
Untraded stock	23.6	48.4	22.1	53.1	a	10.3	25.5	25.6	31.3	39.7
Total	100.0	100.0	100.0	100.0	...	100.0	100.0	100.0	100.0	100.0

Computed from Table A-8.
a Insufficient number of cases.

EFFECTS OF OCCUPATION AND CITY SIZE

OWNERSHIP OF BUSINESS INTEREST STOCKS

The previous analysis suggests that the presence or absence of interest in a business firm with which the investor has a connection other than that of simply supplying capital funds is an important determinant of the manner in which individuals invest their accumulated savings. Farm operators, for example, may invest much of their resources in capital equipment, livestock, and real estate for use in their own operations. Similarly, much of the heavy holdings of untraded stocks by corporate managers may reflect the ownership of stock in corporations which they control. In the case of corporate equity ownership we may test the suggested influence of an interest in the business by measuring the importance of the relevant holdings directly. During the transcription of information from Wisconsin tax returns, notation was made of all dividend receipts from a corporation from which the recipient also received wage or salary income. The holdings of stocks represented by such dividends were termed "business interest" holdings, in order to signify that the owner of such stocks had more than an independent investor's interest in the particular corporation. Generally, the business interest holdings are of three types: holdings by directors, holdings of managers and other corporate executives, and stock owned by rank and file employees.

Table 21 shows the importance of business interest holdings of both traded and untraded stocks at various income levels. While only a little over 10 per cent of the dollar value of the holdings of publicly traded stocks surveyed consists of issues of corporations from which the owner receives wage and salary income, almost two-thirds of the value of untraded stock holdings is comprised of business interest holdings. Moreover, business interest holdings of both traded and untraded stocks increase in importance for successively higher income groups. Because of the significance of this finding, two measures of the extent of business interest holdings of corporate stocks were computed. Whether the measure is the value of the holdings or the amount of dividends received, the results are substantially the same.[3]

The importance of business interest holdings in the case of

[3] The results are subject to two sources of error which may qualify them somewhat. Some individuals failed to itemize sources of wage and salary income, and thus their dividend receipts could not be matched to earnings sources; on the other hand, there may be more complete reporting of dividends from business interest stocks than from other stockholdings.

EFFECTS OF OCCUPATION AND CITY SIZE

TABLE 21

Relative Importance of Business Interest Stock in Holdings of Traded and of Untraded Stock for Income Groups of Wisconsin Individuals, 1949

INCOME	BUSINESS INTEREST STOCK AS A PERCENTAGE OF: Traded Stock Holdings[a]	Untraded Stock Holdings[b]	BUSINESS INTEREST STOCK DIVIDENDS AS A PERCENTAGE OF: Traded Stock Dividends	Untraded Stock Dividends
$0-4,999	2.8%	28.4%	2.3%	32.4%
5,000-9,999	6.0	56.2	5.6	52.0
10,000-19,999	7.3	64.6	5.7	68.0
20,000-49,999	13.8	68.6	10.8	71.2
50,000 and over	36.6	81.3	41.0	80.0
All income groups	11.5%	64.8%	11.5%	66.1%

Based on survey of tax returns. Business interest stocks are those of corporations from which the stockholder received wages, salary, or director's fees.
[a] Based on market value.
[b] Based on unadjusted book value.

untraded stocks strongly suggests that small business places principal reliance for obtaining equity funds on its own management rather than on independent sources. Whatever the importance of the "financial angel" today, the findings here point to the conclusion that a voice in the control of the corporation is probably a necessary, certainly a frequent, cost of "venture" capital for small business. It follows that the reluctance to release even partial control in such enterprises may practically restrain their expansion. Furthermore, to the extent that highly developed technical skills are increasingly necessary in the establishment of new business enterprises capable of competing with large well-established concerns, and insofar as technically skilled individuals tend to be young and without any great stake of their own, there may be reason to believe that the potential starters of new businesses are among those least able to finance such ventures. The implications of this conjecture for the problems of economic growth are obvious.

It may be noted parenthetically that the influence of the investor's business affiliation on his choice of financial assets is apparently not confined to the opportunities and requirements for investment in the particular firm with which he is directly associated. Time after time, the composition of the traded stocks owned by individuals revealed that preference for the stocks of corporations in certain industries was probably determined in good part by the industrial affiliation of the investor himself. Thus, a

EFFECTS OF OCCUPATION AND CITY SIZE

paper mill executive's portfolio might contain not only substantial holdings of stock of his own corporation, but an assortment of minor holdings in timber concerns, suppliers of paper mill machinery and chemicals, paper product firms, and even publishing companies. Architects frequently favored stocks in building material concerns; owners of retail concerns, stocks in corporations whose products they sold. Although this type of behavior is hardly consistent with the usual principle of diversification, it may reveal a deeper rationale. Intelligent investment requires extensive knowledge of the particular corporation, the general industry, and allied fields, obtainable in large measure from active participation in the industry. Consequently the advantages of personal association with an industry exert a strong preferential influence upon the individual's investment behavior.

Size of City

Census figures for 1950 were used to classify Wisconsin individuals according to the size of the city in which they resided. In practice the classifications were adjusted so that suburban areas would be included in the parent cities; no particular attention was paid to strict political subdivisions. That procedure seemed necessary because high income individuals who were important investors were often residents of separately incorporated suburban areas adjoining larger cities, or even of the essentially rural outskirts of large cities. In a few cases adjoining cities were merged and given the population rating of the combined population; thus, Appleton, Neenah, Menasha, Kaukauna, Kimberly, and Little Chute were all combined, as were Two Rivers and Manitowoc; Sheboygan, Sheboygan Falls, and Kohler; Madison, Maple Bluff, and Shorewood Hills; Green Bay and Depere; etc. All of Milwaukee county and the adjoining residential areas in southern Ozaukee county were included in the metropolitan classification.[4] The most striking of the "city combinations" occurred in the case of Superior, which was classified as having a population equal to the combined count of Superior, Wisconsin, and Duluth, Minnesota.

Data on the frequency of ownership of various types of financial assets in the United States according to the size of the city in which

[4] This treatment differs from the practice of the Survey of Consumer Finances of including only the twelve largest cities of the United States and their suburbs under the metropolitan classification. Milwaukee would not be considered a metropolitan area under that classification system.

EFFECTS OF OCCUPATION AND CITY SIZE

the owner resides are provided by the 1949 Survey of Consumer Finances (Table 22). This material indicates that the percentage

TABLE 22

Frequency of Ownership of Liquid Assets and of Corporate Stock for Community Size Groups of Spending Units in the United States, Early 1949

	PERCENTAGE OF UNITS HOLDING:	
SIZE OF COMMUNITY	Liquid Assets[a]	Corporate Stock[b]
Metropolitan	78%	10%
Over 50,000	⎫	8
2,500-49,999	⎬ 71	5
Less than 2,500	⎭	6
Open country	65	10

From "1949 Survey of Consumer Finances," *Federal Reserve Bulletin*, August 1949, Table 16, p. 911, and *ibid.*, October 1949, Table 17, p. 1196.

[a] Includes checking accounts, savings accounts, and U.S. government bonds of all types.

[b] Includes common and preferred stocks of corporations open to investment by the general public.

of spending units holding some type of liquid asset (federal government bonds, savings accounts, checking accounts, etc.) increases steadily for successively larger community size groups. On the other hand, spending units residing either in the open country or in metropolitan areas show the greatest frequency of ownership of corporate stocks open to general public investment—10 per cent. Proportionately fewer units residing in moderate-sized communities hold stock of that type.

Data derived from the Wisconsin tax returns indicate lower ownership frequency of traded or publicly held stocks for rural areas than was found by the country-wide Survey of Consumer Finances; but the undercoverage of the farm population by the tax data, and intersurvey differences in community classification and the components of corporate stock, may partially explain the variation in the two results. Perhaps more important, particularly in Wisconsin the farm population has a high frequency of ownership of stock in cooperatives—assets excluded from our classification of corporate stock. In addition, farm residents, particularly in the upper income classifications, were frequent holders of stock in rural banks. Owing to the absence of price data such securities were usually classified as untraded stock in the present survey, but they were included as corporate stock open to investment by the general public in the Survey of Consumer Finances.

99

EFFECTS OF OCCUPATION AND CITY SIZE

The distribution of the population by community size is important, of course, in explaining the distribution of financial asset holdings as determined from the Wisconsin tax returns. About 50 per cent of the population in Wisconsin lives in rural areas or in cities of less than 10,000 population (Chart 9). This segment of the population contributed one-third of the number of holders of time deposits surveyed, 27 per cent of the holders of traded stock, 38 per cent of the holders of untraded stock, and 47 per cent of the number of holders of direct debt assets.

The distribution in terms of dollar value is quite different. Individuals living in open country and in cities of less than 10,000 held about 40 per cent of the dollar value of time deposits and direct debt assets, but only around 20 per cent of the value of traded and of untraded stocks. At the other extreme, 25 per cent of the population is concentrated in Milwaukee and its environs; while residents there accounted for about that proportion of the number of holders of time deposits, debt instruments, and untraded stocks, they included a considerably greater proportion of the holders of traded stocks (36 per cent). In dollar terms, individuals residing in Milwaukee and its suburbs held time deposits and direct debt assets approximately in proportion to their percentage of the population, but had more than proportionate holdings of untraded and especially of traded corporate stock.

The material in Chart 9, along with the data in Chart 10 showing the composition of financial asset holdings for various city size groups, suggests the following generalizations about the influence of city size on the types of financial investments held by individuals: (1) There is a tendency for direct debt investment, as measured in dollar terms, to be concentrated in rural areas and small towns of less than 10,000 population. (2) The ownership of corporate stock is largely concentrated in urban areas. (3) Traded stock is apparently most important as an outlet for financial investment of individuals in cities of 25,000 and over and in metropolitan areas. (4) Untraded stocks are most important for individual investors in communities of medium size (25,000 to 149,999). These generalizations are confirmed for the most part by Table 23, which shows the composition of financial asset holdings by size of city and by income group. On the whole, the generalizations seem to hold independently of income differences among communities of various sizes.

CHART 9

Community Size Distribution of the Population and of Financial Asset Ownership by Individuals in Wisconsin, 1949

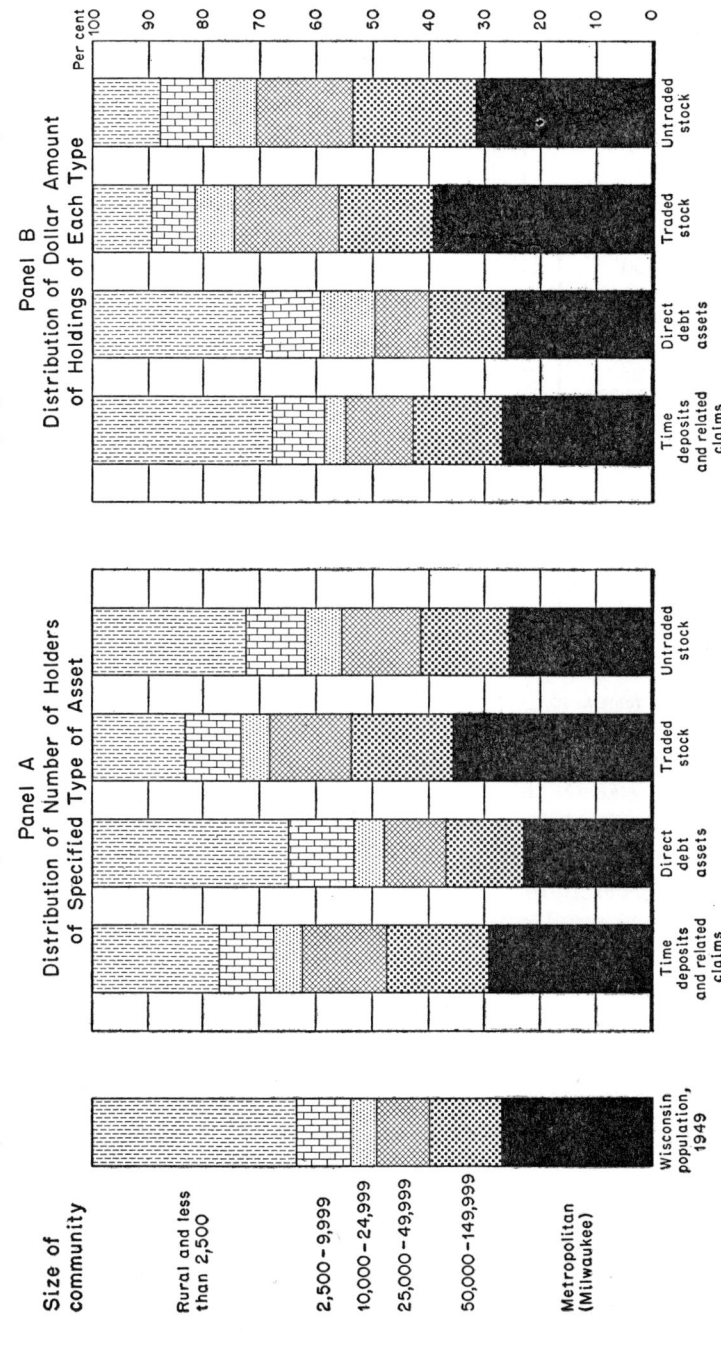

Panel A
Distribution of Number of Holders of Specified Type of Asset

Panel B
Distribution of Dollar Amount of Holdings of Each Type

Panel A from Table A-9, Panel B from Table A-10, and distribution of the population from preliminary data of the Census of Population: 1950.

EFFECTS OF OCCUPATION AND CITY SIZE

CHART 10

Composition of Financial Asset Holdings for Community Size Groups of Wisconsin Individuals, 1949

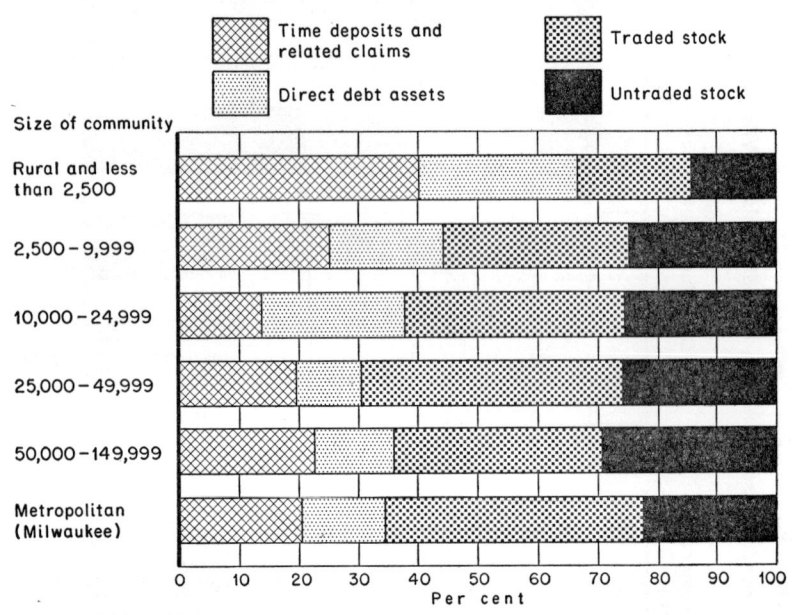

Based on Table A-10.

The findings suggest the general proposition that the influence of city size on the investment practices of individuals, insofar as it is reflected in the distribution of financial assets among the major types, results from the relationship between city size and the typical form of business organization associated therewith. Unincorporated enterprises probably predominate in small towns and rural areas; as a general rule, the corporate form tends to become increasingly important in moderate-sized communities (10,-000 to 24,999), but in middle-sized cities the firms tend predominantly to be closely held corporations of relatively small size. Finally, the industry of metropolitan areas is likely to be characterized by large corporations with traded stock issues.

Such generalizations, if correct, indicate that the form of organization prevalent in a particular size of community has considerable effect upon the form in which the accumulated savings of residents are invested. The financial asset composition of the entire community is probably dominated in part by the investments of persons directly affiliated with business operations, such as man-

EFFECTS OF OCCUPATION AND CITY SIZE

TABLE 23
Composition of Financial Asset Holdings for Wisconsin Individuals Grouped by Size of Community within Income Group, 1949

INCOME GROUP AND TYPE OF ASSET	Less than 25,000[a]	25,000- 149,999	Metropolitan[b]	TOTAL
$0-4,999				
Time dep., etc.	47.6%	44.9%	47.8%	46.9%
Direct debt	29.2	16.7	16.3	22.9
Traded stock	16.9	30.7	29.1	23.3
Untraded stock	6.3	7.7	6.8	6.9
Total	100.0	100.0	100.0	100.0
$5,000-9,999				
Time dep., etc.	22.8	29.5	26.5	26.2
Direct debt	24.7	16.7	18.9	20.2
Traded stock	28.5	34.0	46.3	36.1
Untraded stock	24.0	19.8	8.3	17.5
Total	100.0	100.0	100.0	100.0
$10,000 and over				
Time dep., etc.	6.6	4.9	6.0	5.8
Direct debt	13.8	7.6	11.1	10.6
Traded stock	39.7	40.9	48.6	43.9
Untraded stock	39.9	46.6	34.3	39.7
Total	100.0	100.0	100.0	100.0

Computed from Table A-10.
[a] Includes rural areas.
[b] Includes Milwaukee county and adjoining residential areas in southern Ozaukee county.

agers and self-employed persons, so that the over-all community picture may represent largely the investment activity of that important group. An additional reason for the concentration of traded stock holdings in urban areas is, of course, the general orientation of urban society toward such forms of investment. Thus, the presence of brokerage facilities, the broader newspaper coverage of financial news, and related conditions not only are symptoms of such an interest but tend themselves to promote it. However, there is a considerable tendency toward localization of investment, as the next section will show, even in the case of persons not directly connected with firms in which they invest.

LOCALIZATION OF INVESTMENT

Few restrictions adhere to the mobility of capital funds, at least few in comparison with those which impede the movement of the labor force or other physical production factors. The development of systems of rapid communication and transference of funds, together with the nearly uniform treatment of property rights within modern national economies, greatly facilitates the wide geographic distribution of capital. Although physical capital cannot be transferred easily from one use to another for the economy as a whole, the organization of the capital markets supplies an efficient method whereby the individual investor can shift his own resources from one use to another.

But despite the presence of mechanisms seemingly insuring the geographic mobility of capital funds, a considerable degree of localization of investment is apparent in the ownership of traded corporate stocks (Table 24). In general, one might expect to find investment localization in the ownership of untraded stocks, but it is noteworthy that in the case of traded stocks almost 30 per cent of the value of all holdings by Wisconsin tax filers consisted of stocks in corporations with major operations within the state. In classifying a corporation as a Wisconsin or non-Wisconsin corporation, the principal determination was the location of its operations; little attention was paid either to the particular state of incorporation or to location as determined for tax purposes. No hard and fast rule of what constituted a major portion of a firm's operations was applied; in general, corporations with less than one-third of their employment or plant facilities within the state were treated as out-of-state firms. Chain store companies, railroads, telegraph and telephone systems, and the like were not considered Wisconsin corporations, except in those few cases where their operations were known to be conducted largely in Wisconsin. Certain other nation-wide companies, so regarded because of some degree of geographic diversification of their manufacturing and distribution facilities, were classified as Wisconsin corporations provided one-third of their employment or plant facilities were within the state.

Even after making allowances for the rather broad scope of the survey's definition, the percentage of traded corporate stocks consisting of issues of Wisconsin corporations appears considerably larger than would be expected if no particular tendency for localization of investment existed. The tendency, moreover, is not confined to any one income group: although the highest percentage of traded stock holdings in Wisconsin corporations occurred in the topmost income group, still over one-fourth of the total value of traded

EFFECTS OF OCCUPATION AND CITY SIZE

TABLE 24
Distribution of Traded Stock Holdings by Location of Operations of Issuing Corporation, for Income Groups of Wisconsin Individuals, 1949

STOCKHOLDER'S INCOME GROUP	State of Wisconsin	United States, Other than Wisconsin	Foreign	TOTAL
		All Traded Stock		
$0-4,999	26.3%	70.7%	3.0%	100.0%
5,000-9,999	22.4	77.4	0.2	100.0
10,000-19,999	29.4	70.1	0.5	100.0
20,000-49,999	28.5	71.1	0.4	100.0
50,000 and over	43.7	55.7	0.6	100.0
All income groups	28.3	70.7	1.0	100.0
		Non-business-interest Traded Stock		
$0-4,999	36.6	60.7	2.6	100.0
5,000-9,999	28.4	71.5	0.1	100.0
10,000-19,999	38.2	61.3	0.4	100.0
20,000-49,999	42.7	56.9	0.4	100.0
50,000 and over	44.5	55.0	0.6	100.0
All income groups	37.2	61.9	0.9	100.0

Based on survey of individuals' tax returns.

stocks in the lower income group pertained to issues of Wisconsin corporations.

What is the reason for localization of ownership of traded corporate stocks? Apparently the tendency for individuals to hold stocks of corporations in which they have some business interest does not contribute to the explanation (Table 24). In fact, when business interest holdings are excluded, the proportion (over one-third) of the value of the traded stock holdings relating to issues of Wisconsin corporations is slightly greater than that shown when business interest and other stock holdings are combined. To some extent the localization of stock ownership may come about as a deliberate policy of corporations concerned with community goodwill and employee and customer relations. To some extent the data derived from tax returns may understate the amount of out-of-state holdings of corporate stocks, because taxpayers may believe that dividends from such stock are not taxable or that their omission will not be discovered.

Nevertheless, there is probably good reason to believe that a significant degree of localization of investment exists in the case of traded stocks. Undoubtedly, irrationalities play some part in explaining such localization: to some investors the sight of a corporation's physical assets may prove more reassuring than audited balance sheets and income accounts. Adam Smith, writing about the carrying trade, stated that "every individual endeavours to employ his capital as near home as he can, and consequently as much as he can in the support of domestic industry; provided always that he can thereby obtain the ordinary, or not a great deal less than the ordinary, profits of stock," adding later that this preference was "for the sake of having some part of his capital always under his own view and command."[5] It is likely that some part of the present-day localization of investment in traded corporate stock can be so explained. More important, however, may be the inclination of investment firms—certainly those located outside the primary capital centers—to specialize in certain local issues in the origination and distribution of which they have participated. Thus, it is not surprising that, where yield discrepancies are small, local issues are of considerable importance in the portfolios of their customers.

The principal findings of this chapter are:

1. There are significant differences among occupational groups in the types of financial assets held, both as to frequency of ownership and as to shares of the total dollar value of each type of asset. Most striking is the large proportion of corporate stock held by managerial and self-employed persons.

2. Active interest in business firms with which the investor is closely allied appears to be a major determinant of corporate stock ownership. About two-thirds of the value of untraded stock holdings, but only about one-tenth of the value of traded stocks, represent issues of corporations from which individuals also receive wage or salary income.

3. The influence of community size upon the distribution of financial assets appears to be largely the effect of the form of business organization that is most prevalent in the locality. Thus, in rural areas time deposits and related claims and direct debt assets are most important; in medium-sized cities, where closely held corporations are probably most prevalent, untraded stocks have their greatest importance; in metropolitan areas, characterized

[5] Adam Smith, *An Inquiry into the Nature and Causes of the Wealth of Nations* (Modern Library edition), pp. 421-22.

EFFECTS OF OCCUPATION AND CITY SIZE

by large corporations, traded stocks form a greater proportion of total financial assets than in less urban communities.

4. Investors in corporate stocks appear to have definite preferences for stock of firms located close to their city of residence; about 30 per cent of the value of traded stock held by Wisconsin investors represents stocks of corporations carrying on major operations within the state.

CHAPTER 6

The Characteristics of Traded Stock Holdings

IN PLACING values on holdings of traded stock it was necessary, of course, to identify each separate issue, a step which made possible a number of tabulations designed to answer questions as to who holds various types of stocks. Traded stocks have widely varying characteristics, many of which are related to the safety, liquidity, and earning capacity of an investment, and it is only natural that the preferences of individuals for particular types of issues would also differ. In the belief that an individual's income is not only in itself a significant causative determinant of investment behavior but also closely related to other variables, this chapter is devoted to an analysis of the relation between the composition of portfolios of traded stock and the incomes of holders.

Is it true, for example, that the lower income group, more than individuals with higher incomes, prefers utility stocks and stocks of investment trusts? Which income groups are important holders of bank, oil, iron and steel, and automotive stocks? Does the lower income group hold a greater proportion of its total stockholdings in preferred issues than do higher income groups? Is it possible to distinguish as between income groups different preferences in regard to the quality of stocks? What about differences with respect to diversification practices, yield, price per share, and turnover according to stockholders' income levels? Such questions have practical implications for business finance; their analysis is undertaken in the following sections in the hope of providing additional insight into the characteristics of stock ownership.

Before turning to the findings, however, it should be noted that the various characteristics of stocks are often closely interrelated, with the result that an observed association between income and a particular characteristic may not be independent of relationships with other characteristics of the stock. Thus, the observed preferences of low income individuals for utility stocks may explain their larger-than-average holdings of preferred stocks, since utilities customarily have more preferred shares outstanding than most other types of corporations. Attempts were made to correct for a few such interrelationships, but knowledge of them was too limited to make that possible in all cases.

The Markets in Which Stocks Are Traded

In this section the stock issues held by sampled individuals are divided into three general categories based upon the market facility enjoyed by the particular issue. The categories are: (1) stocks traded on the New York Stock Exchange, (2) stocks traded on the American Stock Exchange (formerly the New York Curb Exchange), and (3) stocks traded on regional exchanges or over the counter. Primarily, this division is adopted because there is an interest on the part of investors and the financial community in the institutional arrangement itself, which interest often extends to speculations about the income characteristics of people owning stocks traded in different markets.

Does the market facility which a stock possesses indicate anything more about the preferences of its holders than merely the institutional arrangement per se? One is inclined to say that it does, for there is some difference between the several exchanges in the types of stocks traded on them as well as a seeming difference in the ease with which the stocks being traded can undergo transfer of ownership. As to differences among the exchanges in the types of firms whose stocks are traded, small firms with ownership largely confined within a region would most frequently have their stocks traded on regional exchanges or over the counter, while the issues of large national concerns with widespread ownership would be found on the New York Stock or the American Stock Exchange. In part these differences arise from the restrictions imposed by the exchanges themselves upon the issues which are granted trading facilities. Perhaps even more important, however, is the apparent arrangement of exchanges into successively higher stages based upon the degree of public interest. To the extent that a high degree of public interest assures an investor of less risk of selling in an imperfect market, the successive market divisions may be taken as indicative of successively higher degrees of ease of liquidation for the particular issues concerned.

But this view is subject to serious reservations. The stock issues which lead in turnover on the regional exchanges and in the over-the-counter market have many times the volume of daily sales that characterizes the inactive stocks traded on the large exchanges. Open-end investment trust stocks, which are traded only over the counter, have immediate liquidation at all times through the issuing company and with the facilities of the over-the-counter market. Moreover, some stock issues are traded on both a regional and a national exchange. The following paragraph, perhaps, gives the best description of the difference between stocks traded on the exchanges and those traded over the counter:

"In general, exchanges provide their broadest markets in issues of substantial size, fairly widely held and having some speculative appeal. The common stock issues of corporations which have moved considerably beyond closely-held local affairs have, as a rule, broad markets on exchanges; so also do the speculative issues among preferreds. This leaves for the over-the-counter market the investment-type preferred issues, certain investment-type common issues and the common issues which are small and fairly closely held and often quite speculative in character. Over-the-counter markets are found in all of these types of issues and frequently constitute either the sole market or the principal one."[1]

While differences between stocks traded on the New York Stock and American Stock Exchanges and those traded over the counter may be fairly sizable, distinctions between those traded on regional exchanges and over the counter are less so. Moreover, the volume of transactions on the regional exchanges is relatively small, and statistical data both for them and for the over-the-counter market are limited. For these reasons stocks traded in the regional markets and stocks traded over the counter were combined, for the analysis, in one category. The decision was perhaps regrettable in view of the recent widespread interest in over-the-counter stocks, but it could not be remedied without considerable difficulty.

As a first indication of intermarket differences in traded stocks Table 25 shows that turnover is considerably slower for issues traded on the regional exchanges and over the counter than for issues traded on the major exchanges. This result probably reflects differences in the degree of public interest, per se, in issues traded in the several markets more than variations in size of issue or corporation, despite the correlation of the last two factors with the intensity of public interest in particular securities.

Of the total value of traded stock held by Wisconsin individuals

[1] G. Wright Hoffman, *Character and Extent of Over-the-Counter Markets* (University of Pennsylvania Press, 1952), p. 16. Despite the differences mentioned, approximately 25 per cent of the common stock issues traded over the counter during the period September through November 1949 were also traded on exchanges. (*Ibid.*)

TRADED STOCK HOLDINGS

TABLE 25

Estimated Turnover of Stocks Traded in Specified Markets and of Untraded Stocks, 1949

Market	Dividend-Paying Stocks Held by Wisconsin Individuals[a]	All Listed Dividend- and Non-dividend-paying Shares[b]
Traded Issues		
New York Stock Exchange	9%	12%
American Stock Exchange	6	7
Regional exchanges and over the counter	4	c
Untraded Issues	4	c

[a] Based on survey of tax returns. Turnover is given as the percentage ratio of the estimated market value of stocks sold by Wisconsin individuals to the estimated value of their stockholdings.

[b] Turnover is given as the percentage ratio of the market value of securities sold to the market value of all listed shares. Data for the New York Stock Exchange compiled from *Statistical Abstract of the United States: 1950*, Tables 481 and 487, pp. 420 and 423; data for the American Stock Exchange, from *ibid.*, Table 487, p. 423, and George L. Leffler, *The Stock Market* (New York, 1951), p. 70.

[c] Not available.

in 1949 about 56 per cent consisted of issues traded on the New York Stock Exchange and about 7 per cent of issues traded on the American Stock Exchange (Table 22).[2] The difficulty of obtaining data on the volume of activity on the regional exchanges and over the counter has led to considerable speculation about the amount of trading done there. In our definition of traded stocks (issues for which 1949 price quotations were available), stocks traded on other than the major exchanges composed about one-third of all traded stocks; if "untraded" issues are included, about three-fifths of the total dollar value of all corporate stocks consisted of issues marketed over the counter or through regional exchanges.[3] This compares roughly with the independent estimate that about one-half of the market value of corporate stocks at the end of

[2] The relationship between the value of stocks traded on the New York Stock Exchange and those traded on the American Exchange may be used as a check on the accuracy of the survey, since the totals can be calculated from market records. The survey of Wisconsin tax returns indicated that 88.7 per cent of the dollar value of stocks traded on the two exchanges consisted of issues traded on the New York Stock Exchange. The comparable figure from the computed totals is 86.2 per cent.

[3] In a few cases, stocks traded both on the regional exchanges or over the counter and on the New York or the American Stock Exchange were classified as traded on the major exchanges.

1949 consisted of issues which find their principal markets over the counter.[4]

Whether one finds large or small differences in the market characteristics of stocks according to the income levels of their holders depends on how one treats untraded stocks. For traded issues, Table 26 shows, the variation as between income groups is not

TABLE 26

Distribution of Traded Stock Holdings According to Market in Which Stock is Traded, for Income Groups of Wisconsin Individuals, 1949

Income	New York Stock Exchange	American Stock Exchange	Regional Exchanges and Over the Counter	Total
$0-4,999	57.4%	9.2%	33.4%	100.0%
5,000-9,999	62.2	3.8	34.0	100.0
10,000-19,999	56.9	6.8	36.3	100.0
20,000-49,999	54.3	6.1	39.6	100.0
50,000 and over	53.6	9.4	37.0	100.0
All income groups[a]	56.3%	7.2%	36.5%	100.0%

Based on survey of individuals' tax returns.

[a] Includes, besides the specified income groups, the small group reporting negative income, for whom the distribution (in the same order as above) was: 44.0%, 8.0%, 48.0%.

very large; but some shift in market characteristics can be noted, as higher income groups are considered, from issues traded on the New York and American Stock Exchanges to those traded on regional exchanges and over the counter. These findings on the market characteristics of stockholdings in the several income groups may be attributable, in part, to real differences in the preferences for securities with varying ease of liquidation. Certainly, securities in active markets can be liquidated more easily than those in less active markets. Although there are many exceptions, stocks traded on the major exchanges have a more active market than those traded on regional exchanges and over the counter. Yet since holdings of business interest stock—many of which pertain to medium and small Wisconsin corporations using local and over-the-counter markets—are more prevalent in higher than in lower income groups, intermarket variation probably cannot be attributed entirely to differences among income groups in liquidity preferences.

Preferred versus Common Issues

Traditionally, preferred stocks are distinguished from common stocks by reference to the contingent claim of the former against

[4] Hoffman, *op. cit.*, p. 11.

the earnings and assets of a corporation and to the residual claims of the latter. Hence preferred stocks have commonly been regarded as falling midway between common stocks and bonds in regard to capital safety, though that view of preferred stocks is difficult to support with empirical evidence. Preferred issues vary widely in quality: some rank with high grade bonds, and others have a dividend claim so large as to eliminate hope of return on common stock, in effect making the preferred issue the residual claimant. Nevertheless, it may be useful to inquire into the relationship between the income levels of stockholders and their holdings of common versus preferred issues, for more important than the intrinsic difference in quality between preferred and common stocks is the question whether investors act as if there were such a distinction.[5]

Table 27 shows a consistent decline for successively higher income groups in the percentage of the market value of traded stock holdings which is composed of preferred issues. The same tendency is found in the case of untraded issues, where value is measured by unadjusted book value. The figures for untraded issues are probably affected somewhat by the fact that a single holder may own both preferred and common issues of the same corporation, a contingency less likely to occur in the case of traded issues. In such cases, except where dividends from common and preferred stocks were specified, a bias existed toward classifying the entire holding as common stock, both because common shares virtually always outnumbered preferred shares and because the dividends that were received on them by some individuals often exceeded the entire dividends paid on preferred shares. Therefore, while the proportions of common to preferred may be incorrect, it is likely that the observed trend for successively higher income groups, away from preferred issues toward common issues, is true of both major classifications of stocks. Accordingly, whatever the

[5] It will be recalled that one of the major difficulties encountered in identifying and valuing traded stocks was to distinguish between common and preferred holdings in the same corporation when both types paid the same dividends per share or when the dividend rates per share on both common and preferred were even multiples of each other. The survey results may be viewed with some confidence since the proportion of the total amount of traded stock held (including over-the-counter securities) consisting of preferred issues—11.4 per cent—compares quite closely with an independent estimate by Goldsmith and Ganz of the percentage of preferreds in the total value of issues traded on the New York Stock Exchange, the American Stock Exchange, and the regional exchanges in 1949—10.7 per cent. (R. W. Goldsmith and Alexander Ganz, "Estimates of Market Value of Corporate Stock: 1900-1949," National Bureau of Economic Research, Capital Requirements Study, Work Memorandum 32, mimeographed, December 1951, Table 1, p. 25.)

TRADED STOCK HOLDINGS

TABLE 27

Distribution of Traded and of Untraded Stock Holdings between Preferred and Common Issues, for Income Groups of Wisconsin Individuals, 1949

INCOME	TRADED STOCK[a] Preferred	Common	TOTAL	UNTRADED STOCK[b] Preferred	Common	TOTAL
$0-4,999	14.7%	85.3%	100.0%	17.9%	82.1%	100.0%
5,000-9,999	13.4	86.6	100.0	8.8	91.2	100.0
10,000-19,999	10.7	89.3	100.0	8.9	91.1	100.0
20,000-49,999	10.5	89.5	100.0	6.0	94.0	100.0
50,000 and over	5.6	94.4	100.0	2.7	97.3	100.0
All income groups[c]	11.4%	88.6%	100.0%	6.7%	93.3%	100.0%

Computed from Table A-11.
[a] Based on market value.
[b] Based on unadjusted book value and includes identifiable issues only.
[c] Includes, besides the specified income groups, the small group reporting negative income, for whom the distributions were as follows. Traded stock: 12.7% preferred, 87.3% common. Untraded stock: 100.0% common.

intrinsic quality differences between common and preferred issues, the lower income group appears to have a greater proportion of its holdings in preferred stock than higher income groups, a result which would be expected if preferred stocks as a class were of better quality than common stocks and if it were assumed that income differences affect attitudes toward quality. The relation between income status and quality of investment will be discussed later. In any case, to some extent one would expect to find relatively high proportions of common issues in the higher income groups because of the importance of the control aspect in holdings of business interest stock.

Industry of Stocks Held

Relationships between the industrial classification of traded stocks and the stockholder's income are shown graphically in Chart 11. Panel A, which shows some types of industry whose issues increase in importance for successively higher income groups, reveals that stocks in wholesale and retail trade concerns, iron and steel, pulp and paper, and nonelectrical machinery are of minor importance in the total market value of traded stock held by the lower income group, but have much greater importance in the higher income groups. Stocks which are important in the portfolios of individuals in the lower income group but which decrease in importance in the upper income groups are shown in Panel B.

TRADED STOCK HOLDINGS

CHART 11

Relative Importance of Stocks of Selected Industries in the Traded Stock Holdings of Income Groups of Wisconsin Individuals, 1949

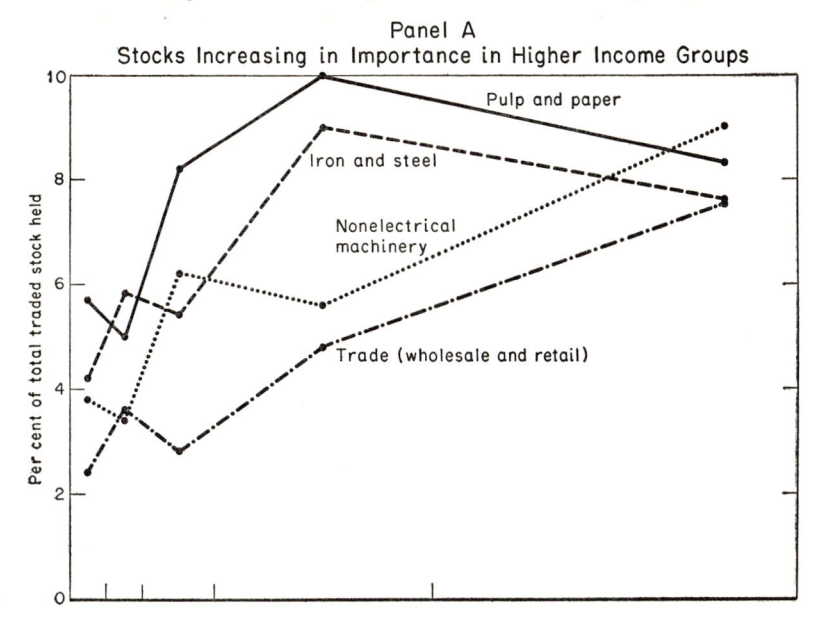

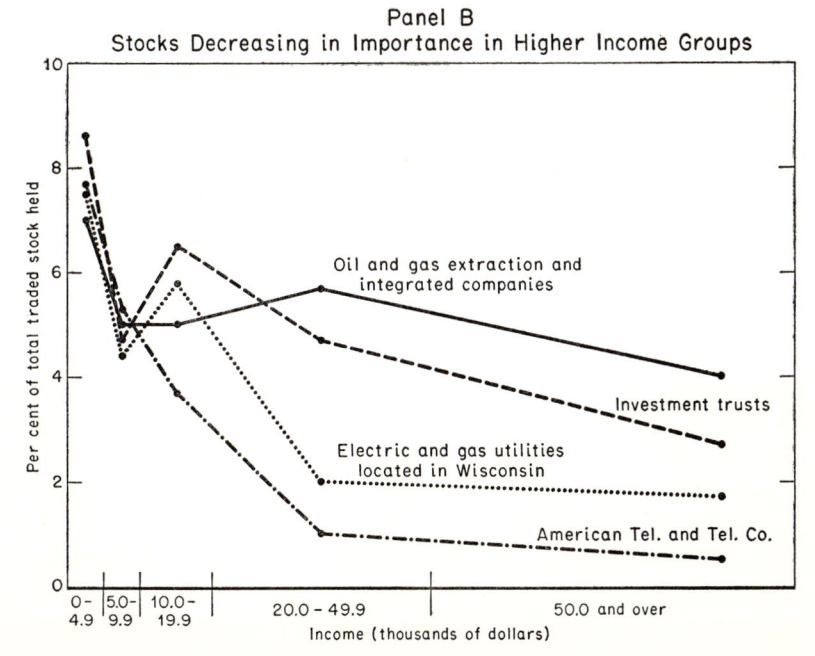

Panel A
Stocks Increasing in Importance in Higher Income Groups

Panel B
Stocks Decreasing in Importance in Higher Income Groups

Based on Table A-12. Readings centered at $90,000 for highest income group and at midpoints of other ranges.

TRADED STOCK HOLDINGS

CHART 11 (continued)

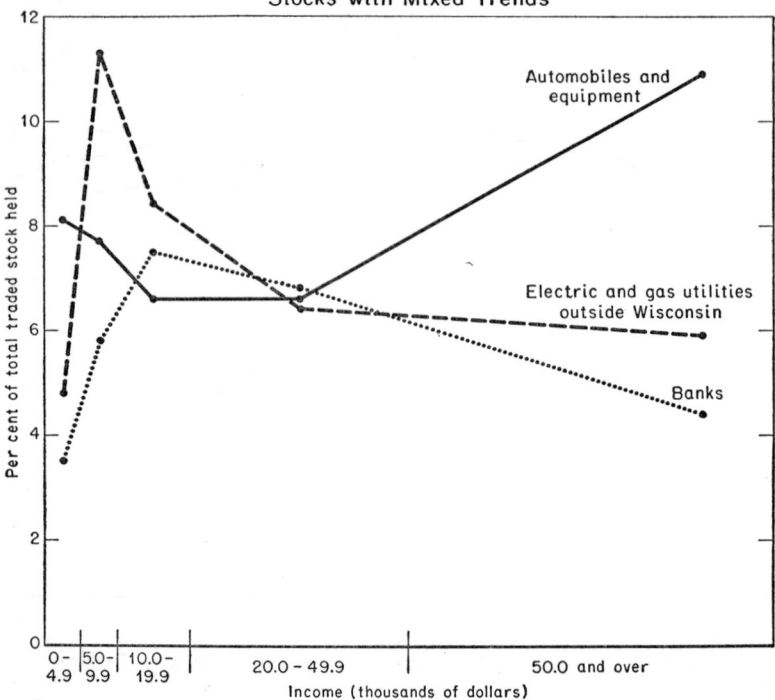

Panel C
Stocks with Mixed Trends

Based on Table A-12. Readings centered at $90,000 for highest income group and at midpoints of other ranges.

Three of the four types of stocks behaving in that way—investment trusts, electrical and gas utilities in Wisconsin, and American Telephone and Telegraph stock—are generally considered to be conservative investments, but the fourth type, petroleum stock, is usually thought of as predominantly speculative. Panel C shows some stocks with mixed trends: bank stocks, for example, increase gradually in importance as income increases until somewhere in the $20,000 income range, where their importance begins to drop off. To some extent, of course, the industrial composition of the traded stock holdings of Wisconsin individuals is a function of the industrial composition of the state of Wisconsin. Thus, relatively large holdings of business interest stocks in the higher income groups would naturally be reflected in relatively large stockholdings in the categories of nonelectrical machinery, iron and steel, and pulp and paper, for these are important industries in the state.

The preference of the lower income group for utility stocks is of considerable interest and importance. Although as a group the utility holdings decrease in importance for successively higher income groups, a mixed trend is observable when electric and gas utilities located in Wisconsin are compared with those outside the state. For the lower income group (under $5,000), stocks of utilities located in Wisconsin are almost twice as important among traded holdings as are stocks of utilities located outside the state, but in the next higher income group ($5,000 to $9,999) the relationship is reversed. Utility firms at one time followed a conscious policy of selling stock rather widely to the lower income groups, particularly to their customers, and some part of the observed distribution of utility stocks may be explained by that policy.[6]

It will be noted that stocks in investment trusts show some evidence of being more important for the lowest than for the high income groups. This would be expected, of course, because their major appeal is that they allow individuals with only small amounts of funds to achieve diversification. But it is interesting to note that these institutions find shareholders throughout the range of incomes: in the higher income groups, individuals with twenty or more different issues were frequently found to be holders of some investment trust stocks.

Table 28 shows the distribution of the book value of holdings of untraded issues by industrial classification and by income group of holder. The make-up of the industry groups for untraded stocks differs somewhat from that for traded stocks; for instance, the transportation group includes mainly transfer companies and local bus lines, whereas in the case of traded stocks it consists predominantly of interstate carriers, such as rails and airlines. Furthermore, the data on holdings of untraded stock cannot be taken as indicative of differential total investment in various industries by different income groups because much of the investment of the lower income group in particular industries takes the form of an interest in unincorporated businesses—for example, unincorporated retail trade concerns.

But that would not be true in the case of untraded bank stocks, which make up a large proportion of the holdings of the low and

[6] See *Financial Policy of Corporations*, by Arthur Stone Dewing (New York, 1941), 4th ed., Vol. II, pp. 1216-20.

TABLE 28

Distribution of Untraded Stock Holdings by Industry of Issuing Corporation, for Income Groups of Wisconsin Individuals, 1949

STOCKHOLDER'S INCOME GROUP	Manufacturing	Retail and Wholesale Trade	Construction	Transportation, Communication, Public Utility	Banking	All Others	TOTAL
$0-4,999	33.0%	7.4%	...	2.0%	40.0%	17.6%	100.0%
5,000-9,999	27.3	24.1	0.4%	0.6	34.8	12.8	100.0
10,000-19,999	53.1	16.1	1.4	2.3	19.2	7.9	100.0
20,000-49,999	56.5	18.6	2.7	2.6	9.8	9.8	100.0
50,000 and over	78.1	4.4	2.0	0.6	4.1	10.8	100.0
All income groups[a]	55.6%	14.7%	1.6%	1.6%	15.8%	10.7%	100.0%

Computed from Table A-13 and includes identifiable issues only.

[a] Includes, besides the specified income groups, the small group reporting negative income, for whom the distribution was: manufacturing, 9.2%; trade, 75.8%; transportation, etc., 2.5%; banking, 12.5%.

TRADED STOCK HOLDINGS

middle income groups. To some extent the prominence of such stocks in their holdings may result from an overestimate, due to confusion on the part of taxpayers as to whether returns on time deposits constituted interest or dividend income. On the other hand, it is a fact that in rural areas local bank stocks are more easily available as an investment outlet than are other types of securities; they are generally regarded as conservative, and the local bank in rural areas looms large as a business. The fact that income levels are somewhat lower in rural communities than in cities and metropolitan areas may partly account for the prominence of bank stocks in the untraded holdings of individuals with lower incomes.

As with traded issues, so with untraded issues the tendency for investment in manufacturing companies to make up a higher proportion of the value of holdings for successively higher income groups is probably due in part to the fact that extremely high incomes arise mainly in manufacturing activities, where business interest holdings are particularly prevalent.

Risk Rating of Stockholdings

It is frequently said that the individual income tax, and particularly its treatment of capital gains and losses, places serious restraints on the willingness of individuals to make investments involving a relatively high degree of risk. Since it is thought that individuals in the lower income group are scarcely in a position to participate at all heavily in this investment function, and that it therefore devolves on the upper income groups, special interest attaches to such information as can be had on the actual practices of high versus low income individuals in choosing among investments with varying degrees of risk. The availability of agency ratings for about 75 per cent of the dollar value of traded stock issues held by Wisconsin individuals permits us to examine the relation between the incomes of stockholders and the quality of at least the major portion of their holdings of traded stocks. The analysis, although it casts no light on what the situation would have been if a progressive income tax had not existed in 1949, may be expected to exhibit preference patterns of different income groups in 1949 with respect to risk taking in one area of investment.

The quality ratings used are those published monthly by the Fitch Publishing Company, based primarily on the stability and prospects of dividends. It is not entirely clear whether or to what

TRADED STOCK HOLDINGS

extent the ratings are also influenced by considerations of stability of market value, where market and dividend prospects differ widely. In any event, the Fitch ratings do not attempt, as do some others, to show whether stocks are over- or underpriced with respect to future prospects. Stocks are classified in twelve categories based on estimates of future dividends. No ratings are assigned to issues of banks, finance companies, investment trusts, etc., because of non-recurring items which affect their operating experience. Small issues, on which data sufficient for rating purposes are unavailable, are also excluded.[7]

Issues of marketed stocks for which Fitch ratings were available were classified according to their December 1949 ratings. Holdings of issues in the three lowest grades (DDD, DD, and D) were virtually nonexistent in the sample: only a very few traded stock issues in 1949 were in financial difficulties and therefore warranted those ratings; as such issues rarely pay dividends, few of them were found in the sample. Because of the small number of such issues and the circumstances surrounding their low ratings, they are ignored in the subsequent analysis. In all, the analysis covers slightly over three-fourths of the total value of traded stock holdings surveyed.

Chart 12 shows as of December 1949 the distribution of the total dollar value of rated stock holdings in each income group according to the Fitch rating grade. The importance of stocks in the four highest grades (AAA, AA, A, and BBB) declines consistently for successively higher income groups. On the other hand, the importance of stocks in the three lowest grades (CCC, CC, and C) decreases to the $20,000 income level and then increases. Furthermore, medium grade issues make up a smaller proportion of the dollar value of rated stock holdings for the lower income group than for others. Because the effect of income level upon the risk aspect of investment choices is not entirely clear, it was thought worth while to devise an index to register the net effect of these trends and the approximate amount of the shifts in quality which are found to occur along the income scale. Such an index is computed by assigning numerical equivalents to each Fitch rating (i.e. AAA equals 1, AA equals 2, A equals 3, BBB equals 4, etc.) and then weighting the dollar value of stockhold-

[7] For a detailed description of the criteria used to assign ratings see *The Fitch Stock Record*, January 1950, p. 6.

TRADED STOCK HOLDINGS

CHART 12

Distribution of Stockholdings by Fitch Agency Rating, 1949, for Income Groups of Wisconsin Individuals

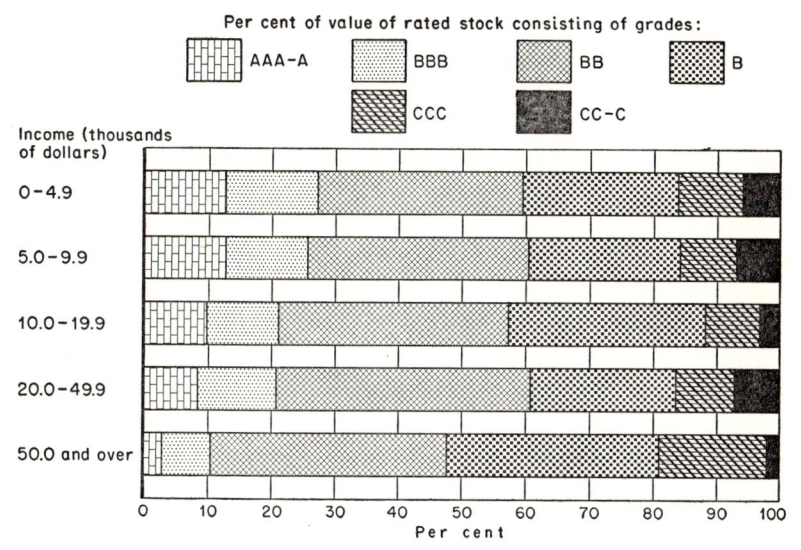

ings of each rating grade by the numerical equivalent for that grade, and aggregating and dividing through by the dollar value of rated stock held for each income group.

The attempt to assess the risk-taking propensities of different individuals is beset with all of the numerous difficulties which the limitations of the sample data involve, especially the absence of information on holdings of non-dividend-paying stocks. In addition, the method used to compute the indexes designed to measure risk taking makes certain assumptions which it is well to review before reporting the findings of the analysis. First, it is necessarily assumed that the risk position of individuals and of income groups is determined solely by their holdings of traded stocks bearing agency ratings. That, however, is an objectionable assumption, since an individual having a bank account and government bonds in addition to CC stock is in a substantially more conservative position than if the CC stock were his only investment. Furthermore, even within the classification of traded stocks, certain issues such as those of banks and investment trusts had no rating and thus were not included in the calculation. But the assumption avoids the knotty problem of ranking assets of different types, such as savings accounts, rated stocks, and closely held stocks, on the same quality scale.

The second assumption is somewhat more technical: a linear arithmetic relationship is assumed to exist between agency rating grade and true quality. Thus, it is assumed that the difference in quality between BBB and BB stocks is the same as between BB and B stocks, so that not only do agency ratings serve to rank the various issues of stock according to quality but the successive ratings bear a constant quantitative relationship to each other. We clearly do not know whether the assumption is valid or not, because no objective measure of risk exists with which agency rating grades can be compared. If the relationship of current dividends to market price (i.e. yield) is used as a standard of comparison in the belief that successively poorer grades of stock bear successively higher yields, the assumption appears to be untrue because the relation between yield and agency rating does not appear to be linear. A tentative explanation of the nonlinearity of the relationship will be advanced in a later section.

The practical importance of this assumption, that the relationship between agency rating grade and true quality is one of arithmetic linearity, is evident when one considers the method of constructing measurements of risk taking. If an individual or an income group has $1,000 in BBB stocks and a like amount in B stocks, the true average risk of the individual or group will be BB only if the difference between BBB and BB stocks is equivalent to the difference between BB and B stocks, absolute risk levels notwithstanding. Since in computing indexes a constant arithmetic scale was used to signify varying grades of risk, the stated assumption is implicit in the analysis. To make any other assumption would require more evidence than is presently available.

Chart 13 shows the behavior of the quality index. There is a fairly constant downward trend in the average agency rating grade, symbolizing a general decline in quality of stockholdings as income increases. The decline in quality of stockholdings for successively higher income is not as great, however, as might be expected: the net difference in quality of aggregate portfolios of rated stocks between the lowest and highest income groups is only about two-fifths of one rating grade.

One possible reason that we do not find greater differences in risk propensities between income groups is that many small holders

CHART 13
Relationship between Income Level and Quality of Holdings for Wisconsin Individuals Owning Traded Stock, 1949

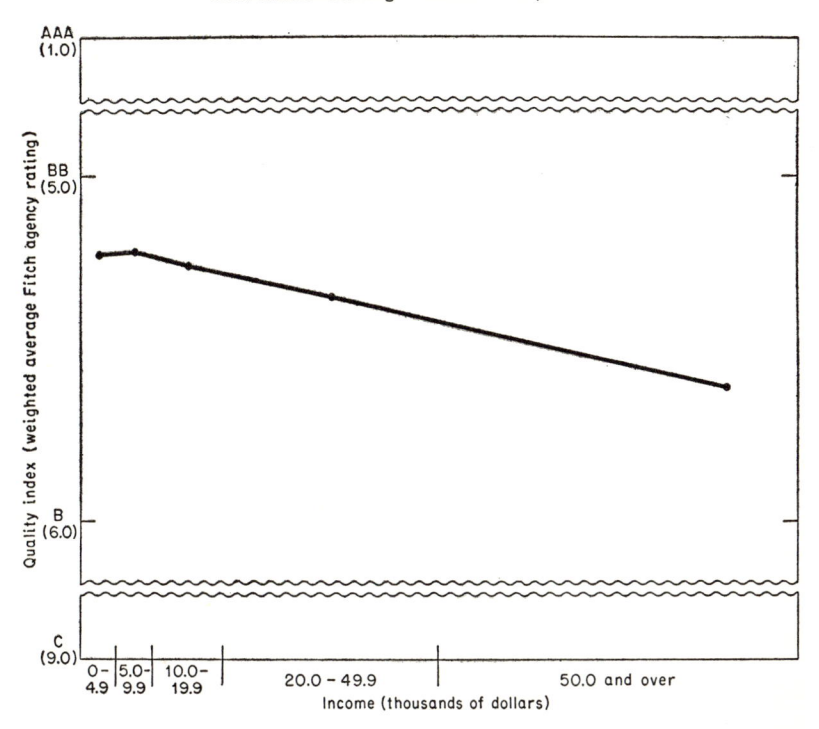

Based on Table A-14. Readings centered at midpoints of income class intervals, except that for the $50,000 and over class the approximate mean, $90,000, is used.

of stock appear to hold relatively risky positions and that small holders make up a larger proportion of all stockholders in the lower income group than in the upper ones. In Chart 14 the individuals in the several income groups have been classified as to risk position by a quality coefficient calculated separately for each stockholder. This procedure weights each stockholder equally regardless of the amount of rated stock held. Average quality coefficients were computed for different size-of-holding groups within income groups, to allow the examination of the effect of income independently of the effect of size of stockholdings. In general, within each subgroup of investors having the same amount of traded stocks, the higher the income level the lower is the average rating grade, symbolizing a decline in quality—a greater assumption of risk—as income rises. This relationship is most nearly con-

TRADED STOCK HOLDINGS

CHART 14

Relationship between Income Level and Risk Position for Wisconsin Individuals Grouped by Size of Holding of Traded Stocks, 1949

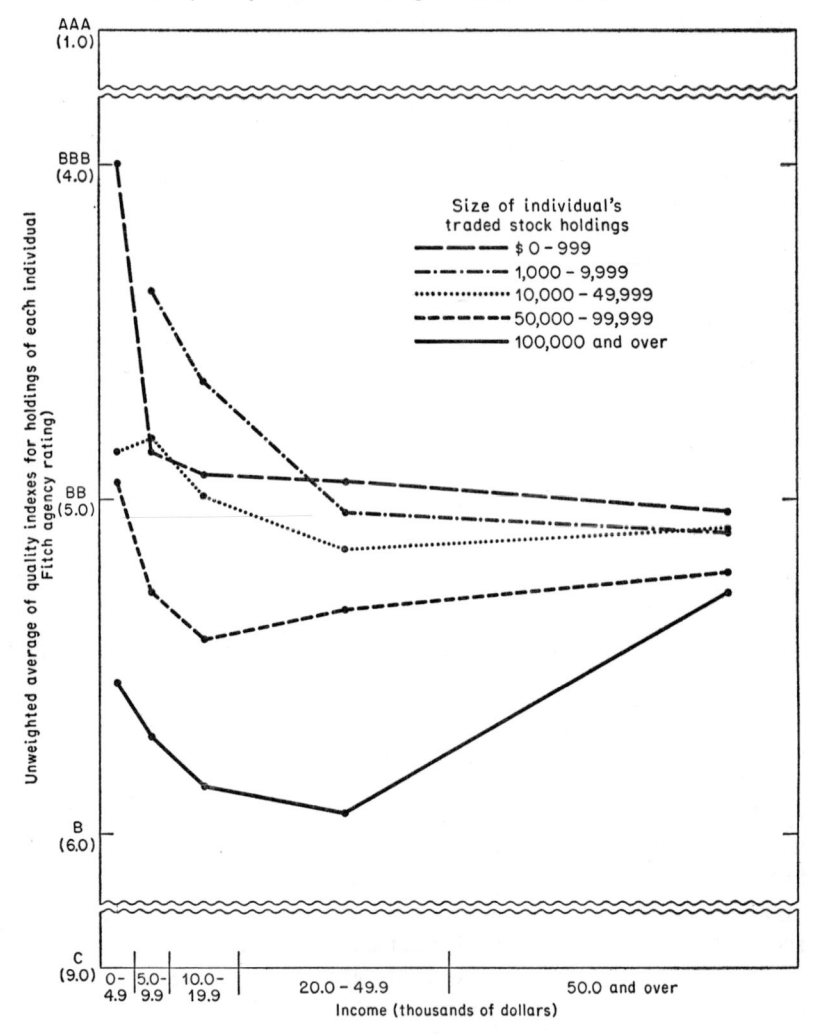

Based on survey of tax returns. Readings are centered at midpoints of income class intervals, except that for the $50,000 and over class the approximate mean, $90,000, is used.

sistent in the case of stockholders with incomes of less than $50,-000; beyond that level the average risk decreases for individuals holding less than $50,000 of traded stocks. Within any single income group, however, average risk is generally higher for in-

124

dividuals holding small amounts of traded stocks than for those with larger holdings.

This last finding—that individuals with small amounts of traded stock holdings have positions of greater risk, on the average, than individuals with larger holdings, income held constant—is of considerable interest. One might expect to find small holders choosing very conservative investments and large holders within the same income groups holding riskier investments. Yet economic literature and experience abound with illustrations of individuals risking small amounts in the hope of large gains.[8] Lotteries are frequently justified on the basis that they give a poor man an opportunity to take such risks. It is not unlikely that the stock market has a similar appeal to certain persons and that these individuals are of some numerical significance in the low income groups, although the aggregate dollar value of their holdings is slight compared with that of more conservative investors in the same income stratum. Any generalization about the influence of the income level of individuals upon their propensity to assume risk is probably incomplete without acknowledging the fact that the lower and middle income groups contain proportionately more individuals with extremely risky or extremely conservative investment positions than the higher income groups do. This is shown in Chart 15.

In summary, the analysis of the relation between the income level of an individual and his risk position with traded stock holdings suggests that the highest income group holds relatively greater amounts of stock involving higher-than-average risk than any other income group. The fact that the over-all difference in risk position between the lowest and highest income groups is not great may be due to any number of circumstances: the effect of the income tax; the fact that many of the small holders of traded stocks who are relatively numerous in the lower income group appear to hold positions more speculative than the average; or the fact that certain conservative stocks which are primarily concentrated in the lower income group, such as stocks of investment trusts, were not rated and therefore were excluded from measurement.

Diversification

How many different issues are held by the average stockholder and how does diversification vary with income?

[8] For a recent theoretical discussion of this phenomenon see "The Utility Analysis of Choices Involving Risk," by Milton Friedman and L. J. Savage, *Journal of Political Economy*, August 1948, pp. 279-304.

TRADED STOCK HOLDINGS

CHART 15
Distribution of Holders of Rated Stock by Risk Position, for Income Groups of Wisconsin Individuals, 1949

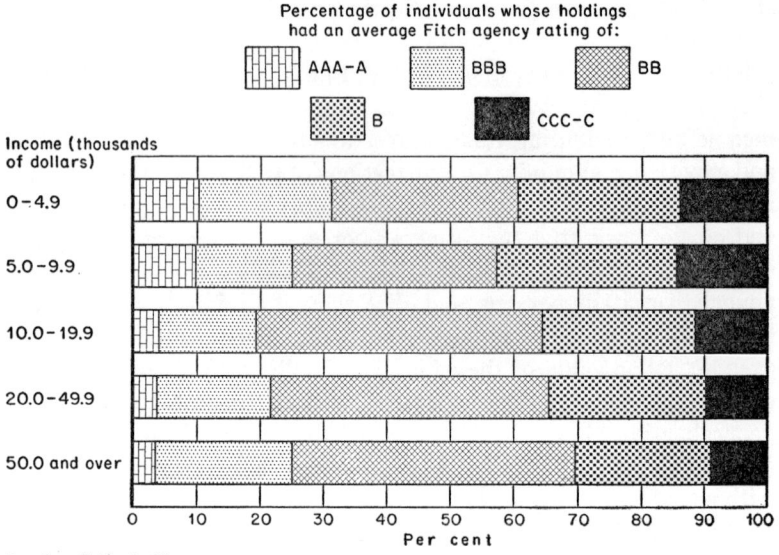

Percentage of individuals whose holdings had an average Fitch agency rating of:
AAA-A   BBB   BB   B   CCC-C

Income (thousands of dollars)
- 0-4.9
- 5.0-9.9
- 10.0-19.9
- 20.0-49.9
- 50.0 and over

Per cent

Based on Table A-15.

In measuring degree of diversification, number of issues rather than number of corporations in which stocks were held was the criterion used, though it involved counting twice those corporations in which an individual held two classes of stock. If both husband and wife had holdings in the same issue these were counted but once, despite the fact that they might be two separate and distinct holdings.

The average number of issues held, as well as the percentage of holders with only one issue, is shown in Table 29 for income groups and also for groups of individuals ranked according to the amount of their holdings of traded stocks. The average number of traded issues held increases both with income and with size of holding, except that there is a slight drop in the average in the highest class.

It should be pointed out, however, that indications from the Wisconsin income tax returns on the average number of issues held were high as compared with those of other surveys. The 1949 Survey of Consumer Finances, for example, found that "roughly half of the spending units who reported owning [publicly traded] stock stated that they had invested in only one corporation; ap-

TRADED STOCK HOLDINGS

TABLE 29

Relation of Average Number of Issues Held, and of Percentage of Holders with Only One Issue, to Income Level and Size of Holding for Wisconsin Individuals Owning Traded Stock, 1949

Characteristics of Holder	Average Number of Issues Held	Percentage of Holders with Only One Issue
Income		
$0-4,999	3.8	43.6%
5,000-9,999	5.5	35.1
10,000-19,999	9.4	26.0
20,000-49,999	12.5	16.5
50,000 and over	18.1	13.7
Size of Traded Stock Holdings		
$1-499	1.2	86.1
500-999	1.6	56.0
1,000-4,999	2.8	31.5
5,000-9,999	5.6	10.5
10,000-19,999	9.1	10.7
20,000-49,999	15.0	1.2
50,000-99,999	21.7	1.0
100,000-999,999	39.3	5.5
1,000,000 and over	35.0	0
All holders of traded stock[a]	5.4	38.3%

Based on survey of tax returns.

[a] Includes individuals reporting negative income, for whom the average number of issues was 14.9 and the proportion with only one issue 25.0%.

proximately one-third held stock in from 2 to 10 corporations; and less than one-tenth owned shares in 11 or more corporations."[9] In comparison, the Wisconsin data show that 38 per cent of the tax filers reporting ownership of traded stock held only one issue, almost half held 2 to 10 issues, and about 12 per cent held more than 10 issues.

But both of those surveys indicated greater diversification than appeared in a Treasury survey of federal income tax returns for 1936, which found that 62 per cent of the stockholders with net incomes over $1,000 or $2,500 (depending on marital status) and under $5,000 received dividends from one corporation, 34 per cent from 2 to 9 corporations, and about 4 per cent from 10 or more corporations.[10] The Treasury survey was confined, however,

[9] "1949 Survey of Consumer Finances," *Federal Reserve Bulletin*, October 1949, p. 1191.
[10] *The Distribution of Ownership in the 200 Largest Nonfinancial Corporations* (Temporary National Economic Committee Monograph 29, 1940), p. 12.

to individuals receiving net incomes of less than $5,000 and dividends of less than $10,000.

Yield

There is a considerable body of evidence which suggests that the relation between stock yields and quality, as ordinarily measured, is not always one of simple linearity. In other words, one cannot say that the best grade of stock has the lowest yield, intermediate grades have somewhat higher yields, and the riskiest stocks the greatest yields. On the contrary, while yields increase from the prime to the intermediate grades of traded stock, the poorest grades appear actually to pay lower yields (in terms of the ratio of dividends to market value) than do issues of intermediate quality.

This relationship is shown in Chart 16 for the sample of dividend-paying stocks held by Wisconsin individuals in 1949. The irregular variations which will be noted in the yields of high quality stocks are doubtless due to the small number of cases in some of these groups, but the decline in yields on stocks with ratings lower than B is sufficiently regular in shape to warrant confidence that it reveals a true condition. This backward-turning yield curve, moreover, is not simply a phenomenon unique to the Wisconsin sample; on the contrary, it appears to be characteristic of stock listings for 1949 taken at random from the investment manuals. Furthermore, it appears to be true of stocks traded on the regional exchanges and over the counter as well as of those traded on the major exchanges, although more of the former group fall in the extreme right-hand segment of the curve.[11]

The reason for this behavior is not easy to discern. Stocks of the poorest grades show much greater diversity of yield than do medium and high grade stocks. On the one hand, low grade issues include stocks of firms whose growth possibilities are comparatively severely limited to the occurrence of chance events, such as mineral discoveries. For the most part those appear to be high-yielding securities. On the other hand, also among the low grade issues are

[11] Friedman and Savage suggest that the presence of individuals desiring high returns on their investments in numbers that are large in relation to the supply of investments offering such chances may result in higher returns for moderately risky assets than for assets having either little or much risk, essentially the condition suggested by the backward-turning yield curve in Chart 16. (*Op. cit.*, p. 301.)

CHART 16
Relationship between the Quality and Yield of Rated Stock Holdings of Wisconsin Individuals, 1949

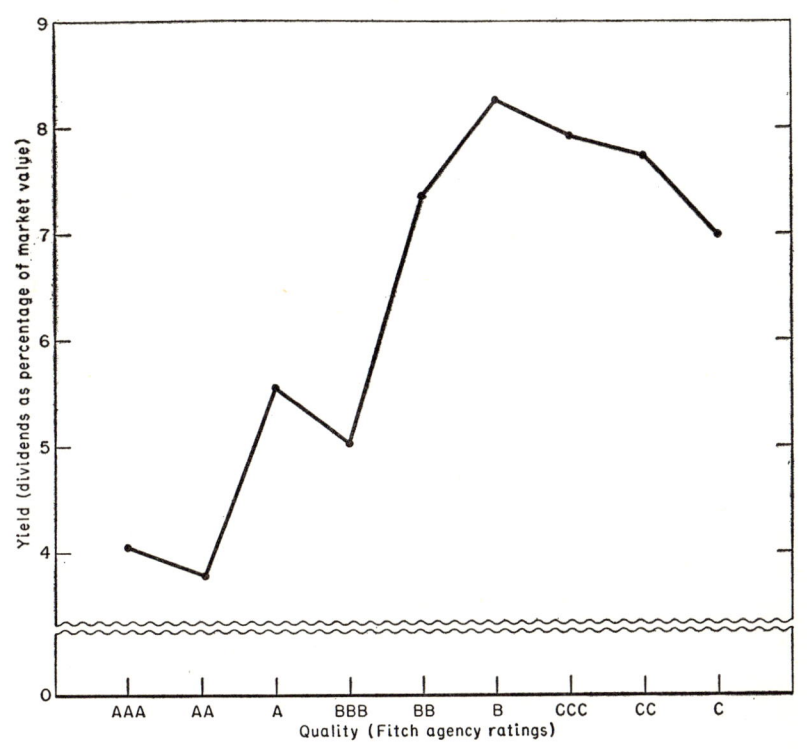

Based on survey of tax returns.

stocks of young industries such as television, though these have extremely low yields if the ratio of dividends to market price is the measure used. Some bias may have been introduced into the analysis by the fact that corporations encountering financial difficulties may immediately cease to make dividend payments, while new firms with shaky finances but prospects for growth may find it expedient to make small dividend payments in order to safeguard their record in case future external financing is sought. Thus, our sample of low grade, dividend-paying stocks would have a bias toward issues of new firms with growth possibilities but with small current dividend yields. Although it cannot be determined from the data whether low grade stocks are commonly overpriced as compared with intermediate and high grade stocks, it would appear in any event that the market, at least in 1949, was more optimistic about such issues than the rating agencies were.[12]

Investigation of the relation between investors' incomes and the yields from their holdings of equity securities is considerably hampered by the fact that yields for the sample have been measured as of 1949, whereas yield might well be measured for a period longer than a year and possibly should be defined so as to take into consideration any realized or unrealized gains or losses occurring since the purchase date as a result of changes in capital values.

As an illustration of this last point it may be well to examine one feature of the current income tax structure. It has been suggested that the liberal provisions regarding taxation of long-term capital gains will encourage high income individuals to purchase the stocks of corporations which retain most of their earnings. The argument assumes, of course, that market price will rise proportionately with the rise in book value occasioned by the retention of earnings. If the tax treatment of capital gains were important, as has been suggested, in determining the behavior of investors, one would expect yields figured as the ratio of dividends to the value of stock held to decline for successively higher income groups. Table 30 appears to confirm that thesis except in the case of individuals with incomes of $50,000 or over, for whom the yield on traded stocks is higher than for any other group. One would expect persons in the top income group to be benefited most by the provisions of the capital gains tax; accordingly, the presence of extremely high yields on the marketed stocks held by that group casts doubt upon the validity of the thesis as a sole explanation of investor behavior. At least some part of the irregular behavior of the average yield obtained by individuals in the top income groups is probably associated with the phenomenon of the backward-turning yield curve, since the holdings of stock by the highest income group could not produce a yield higher than the average for all income groups unless they included issues with rating grades having the highest average yields—i.e. not the riskiest but the moderately risky stocks.

With untraded stocks the difficulty in determining actual yields

[12] A somewhat similar condition appears to prevail in the market for farm land. Several studies indicate that land poorly adapted to the type of farming carried on in the area is valued higher in relation to financial returns than well-adapted land. See *Mortgage Lending Experience in Agriculture*, by Lawrence A. Jones and David Durand (Princeton University Press for the National Bureau of Economic Research, 1954), Chapters 8 and 9.

TRADED STOCK HOLDINGS

TABLE 30

Yields of Traded and of Untraded Stock Held, for
Income Groups of Wisconsin Individuals, 1949

INCOME	TRADED STOCK[a] Preferred	Common	ALL TRADED	UNTRADED STOCK[b] Preferred	Common	ALL UN-TRADED
$0-4,999	5.13%	7.28%	6.97%	3.92%	3.21%	3.34%
5,000-9,999	4.80	6.83	6.56	7.55	3.10	3.49
10,000-19,999	4.94	6.70	6.51	5.09	4.26	4.33
20,000-49,999	4.61	6.47	6.28	5.69	4.92	4.97
50,000 and over	4.34	7.31	7.15	6.12	5.10	5.12
All income groups[c]	4.84%	6.87%	6.63%	5.49%	4.57%	4.63%

Computed from Table A-11. Yields are expressed as the percentage ratio of dividends to market or book value of stock.
[a] Based on market value.
[b] Based on unadjusted book value and includes identifiable issues only.
[c] Includes, besides the specified income groups, the small group reporting negative income, for whom the yields on traded stock were: preferred, 4.42%; common, 5.63%; all, 5.48%. All untraded stocks held by this group were common stocks, the average yield being 7.35%.

is even greater than for traded stocks, since the yield on the investment is obscured by the fact that about two-thirds of the value of such stock is owned by individuals also receiving wages or salaries from the issuing corporation.[13] In many such cases it is impossible to separate wages of management from profits received in the form of dividends; one would expect, nevertheless, that if the possibility of avoiding high personal tax rates through retention of earnings were influencing investor practice the evidence would be found most clearly in holdings of stock in closely held corporations. Instead, as Table 30 shows, higher income individuals received a higher yield on their untraded stock than did lower income individuals.

Average Turnover of Holdings

The data available from the capital gains and losses schedule of the tax returns make it possible to measure the market activity of different economic groups. The measure is one-sided in that only sales are recorded, but it may be presumed that under normal circumstances most investors sell in order to acquire another asset, frequently to buy another stock. In certain cases that is not so,

[13] The levels of yields received on traded and untraded stocks are not comparable, since unadjusted book value was used to compute the yield on untraded stocks. Adjustment to market value equivalent considerably raises the yield indicated for untraded stock but does not substantially change the differences between income groups.

of course: for example, older investors may be net sellers, on balance, while younger individuals may be net purchasers. These would tend to be offsetting conditions, however, and figures on turnover computed from sales information as listed in the capital gains schedules of the tax returns may give at least a rough indication of market activity.

The average turnover for different income groups of stockholders may be measured by dividing the total sales price of stocks sold by them during 1949 by the total value of their average holdings of stocks. Thus we obtain for each group the percentage of average holdings sold during the year. Such a measure of turnover lacks precision for two reasons: First, stocks that are sold are valued at their actual sales price, while average holdings are computed at the unweighted mean market price during 1949. Second, average holdings are estimated only for stocks paying dividends during 1949, while the sales figure includes marketed stocks which did not pay a return to the investor. In short, the concepts of valuation in the numerator and denominator differ somewhat, and one small class of stocks is represented only in the numerator.

Table 31 reveals that traded stocks sold during 1949 represented

TABLE 31

Estimated Turnover of Traded Stock Holdings for Income Groups of Wisconsin Individuals, 1949

Income	Turnover
$0-4,999	6.6%
5,000-9,999	8.5
10,000-19,999	8.1
20,000-49,999	6.9
50,000 and over	4.1
All income groups[a]	6.7%

Computed from Tables A-3 and A-16. Turnover is the percentage ratio of the sales price of traded stocks sold during the year to the average market value of traded stock holdings, 1949.

[a] Includes, besides the specified income groups, the small group reporting negative income, for whom turnover was 3.9%.

only about 7 per cent of the average total value of such stocks held by Wisconsin individuals filing tax returns for that year. The comparable figure for untraded stocks was 4 per cent. Average turnover of traded stock was slightly higher for individuals having incomes of from $5,000 to $19,999 than for income groups above or below that range. According to 1949 data, individuals with incomes of $50,000 and over had the lowest rate of traded stock turnover of any income group.[14]

In 1949 one-third of the value of traded stocks sold was comprised of issues which had been held for less than one year, and such briefly held securities made up a larger part of sales for the income group under $5,000 than for others (Table 32). Par-

TABLE 32

Distribution of Traded Stock Holdings Sold in 1949 by Length of Time Held, for Income Groups of Wisconsin Individuals

LENGTH OF TIME HELD	$0-4,999	$5,000-9,999	$10,000 & Over	ALL INCOME GROUPS
6 months and under	18.6%	14.9%	13.7%	14.7%
6 months to 1 year	26.1	27.3	14.1	19.3
1 to 2 years	32.1	21.9	29.6	27.5
2 to 5 years	17.2	12.5	21.6	20.3
5 to 10 years	4.5	7.0	12.4	9.1
Over 10 years	1.5	16.4	8.6	9.1
Total	100.0%	100.0%	100.0%	100.0%

Computed from Table A-16.

ticularly noticeable is the fact that about 20 per cent of the value of stock sold by the upper income group ($10,000 and over) represented issues which had been held five or more years, whereas the comparable figure for the lower income group was only 6 per cent.

In summary, the data show that average turnover is slightly greater in the income ranges below the $50,000 level than above it, and that successively higher income groups tend to hold shares for longer periods of time. Turnover figures, of course, are greatly influenced by a relatively few persons who constantly trade in and

[14] There are considerable differences in turnover among stocks of different agency rating grade. The prime risk issues had the lowest turnover and the relatively risky shares the highest. The turnover for each agency rating grade for all stockholdings in the Wisconsin sample was as follows:

AAA—None BBB—5.0% CCC— 8.6%
AA —None BB —6.6   CC —17.1
A —6.0%   B —7.8   C —23.6

This finding compares roughly with a tabulation of reported turnover of stocks traded on the New York Stock Exchange in 1948 by agency rating grade prepared for the Securities and Exchange Commission. Turnover of stocks in the Wisconsin sample was somewhat smaller than that found by the SEC tabulation, except in the case of stocks of grade A.

out of the market, yet whose holdings at any one time may not be large. Thus, sales by a small number of active traders in the low and medium income groups may bulk somewhat larger in relation to the total holdings of those groups than do sales by a larger number of less active traders in the higher income groups when compared with the group's holdings. In addition, one would expect to find in the topmost income group less pressure for liquidation because of unforeseen emergencies than in the low and middle groups, and greater incentive for holding shares over a somewhat longer period because of the desire to obtain long-term gains.

Price per Share

Do individuals in the lower income groups have a greater preference for comparatively low-priced shares than individuals with higher incomes? This is a question of some practical interest and importance because if price preferences appear to be associated with income levels, their relationship might warrant some attention in designing new security issues to appeal to a particular stratum of society. Furthermore, the relationship between absolute price level of corporate stock shares and income level of holder, if significant, may have implications for problems involving price movements of particular issues. For example, a stock split may lead to a different distribution of stock among income stratifications of stockholders which would also have some effect upon price per share as revealed in a comparison of the new with the previous price, the latter having been adjusted to reflect the split. Similarly, the observed tendency for low-priced shares to rise more in a bull market and decline more in a bear market than medium- and high-priced shares[15] may be associated with changes in the market activity of the lower income groups, if these groups do, in fact, prefer low-priced stocks. Therefore an investigation of the relationship between income level of holder and price per share of stocks held appears warranted.

Chart 17 shows the distribution of Wisconsin stockholders in

[15] This principle, which has been termed the "square root rule," is discussed by Zenon Szatrowski in "The Relationship between Price Change and Price Level for Common Stocks," *Journal of the American Statistical Association*, December 1945, pp. 467-83. It has been pointed out, however, that quality rather than price per share seems to be the major determinant of the degree of fluctuation in stock prices. See "Quality versus Price as Factors Influencing Common Stock Price Fluctuations," by John C. Clendenin, *Journal of Finance*, December 1951, pp. 398-405.

TRADED STOCK HOLDINGS

various income ranges according to the average price per share of their traded stock holdings. As individuals with progressively higher incomes are considered, the proportion who have holdings with either an extremely low or an extremely high average price per share appears smaller. In other words, a relatively greater number of individuals in the higher income groups have stockholdings with moderate average price per share ($20.00 to $49.99) than

CHART 17
Distribution of Holders of Traded Stock by Average Price per Share of Their Holdings, 1949, for Income Groups of Wisconsin Individuals

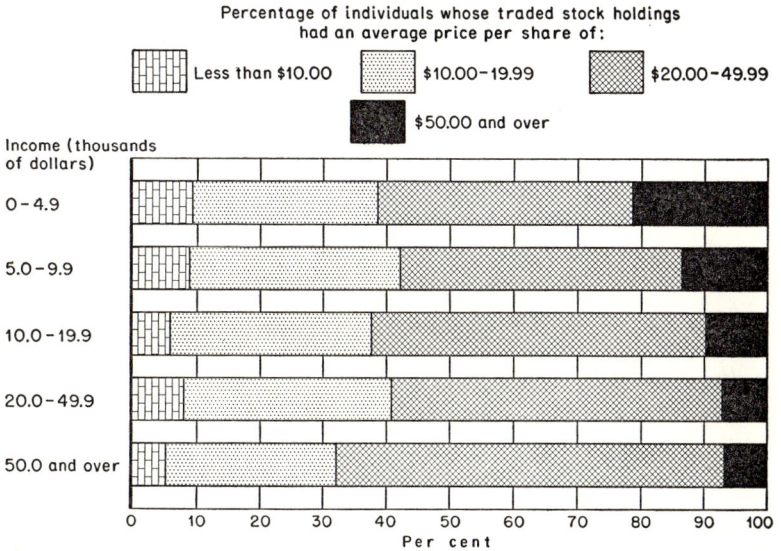

Percentage of individuals whose traded stock holdings had an average price per share of:

- Less than $10.00
- $10.00-19.99
- $20.00-49.99
- $50.00 and over

Income (thousands of dollars)
0-4.9
5.0-9.9
10.0-19.9
20.0-49.9
50.0 and over

Per cent

Based on Table A-17.

in the lower and middle income groups. The complement of that tendency—i.e. a decline, with rise of income level, in the proportionate number of persons having shareholdings in other price-per-share ranges—is not confined to the low price-per-share component alone; in fact, the decline in the case of holdings with high average price per share ($50 and over) is considerably more impressive.

It is not easy to explain these findings, but one may hazard a guess on two factors which may jointly be important. In the first place, there is a close association between the price per share of a stock issue and its quality. As a rule, prime risk stocks sell at relatively high prices per share while progressively lower grades of stocks have progressively lower prices per share. Secondly, as was pointed out earlier, somewhat sizable proportions of individuals in the lower and middle income groups hold either extremely speculative or extremely conservative positions in regard to their stockholdings, whereas progressively higher income groups appear to be characterized by proportionately fewer individuals holding either extremely risky or extremely safe positions. Because of the correlation between quality and price per share, we would expect this tendency for reduced extremes in risk position at higher income levels to be manifested in reduced extremes in the distribution of individuals according to the average price per share of their stockholdings. Essentially that is what is observed in Chart 17.

If the surmise just stated is correct, the analysis should advance one step further into an examination of the relationship between income level and average price per share for stocks of similar quality. Thus one might determine whether it is merely the variation among income groups in the quality of stock held which accounts for differences in average price per share of stockholdings, or whether there is a price effect independent of quality. Chart 18 shows the average price per share of stocks with different Fitch ratings for various income levels. Because of the small number of observations for either extremely safe or extremely risky stocks, the two highest and the two lowest grades have been combined. For the better quality stocks it is difficult to generalize about the effect of income upon average price per share; if anything, the highest income group ($50,000 and over) more than other groups appears to favor the lower-priced stocks among high grade issues. For stock of average quality (BB), price per share appears to be nearly constant at all income levels. It is only with low grade stocks that the low income group appears to prefer, more than higher income groups do, issues selling at a relatively low price per share.

Again it is difficult to explain what is observed. One explanation which seems to fit the facts is that some of the individuals in the lower income group whose position in regard to their stockholdings is relatively speculative not only desire the poorest quality stocks because of their large potential appreciation possibilities but also choose, from among the speculative stocks, those with a low price per share, because of a belief that appreciation possibilities for such issues are even greater—in short, that some individuals seek

TRADED STOCK HOLDINGS

CHART 18

Relationship between Income Level of Holder and Price per Share of Wisconsin Individuals' Holdings, 1949, for Stocks of Different Rating Grade

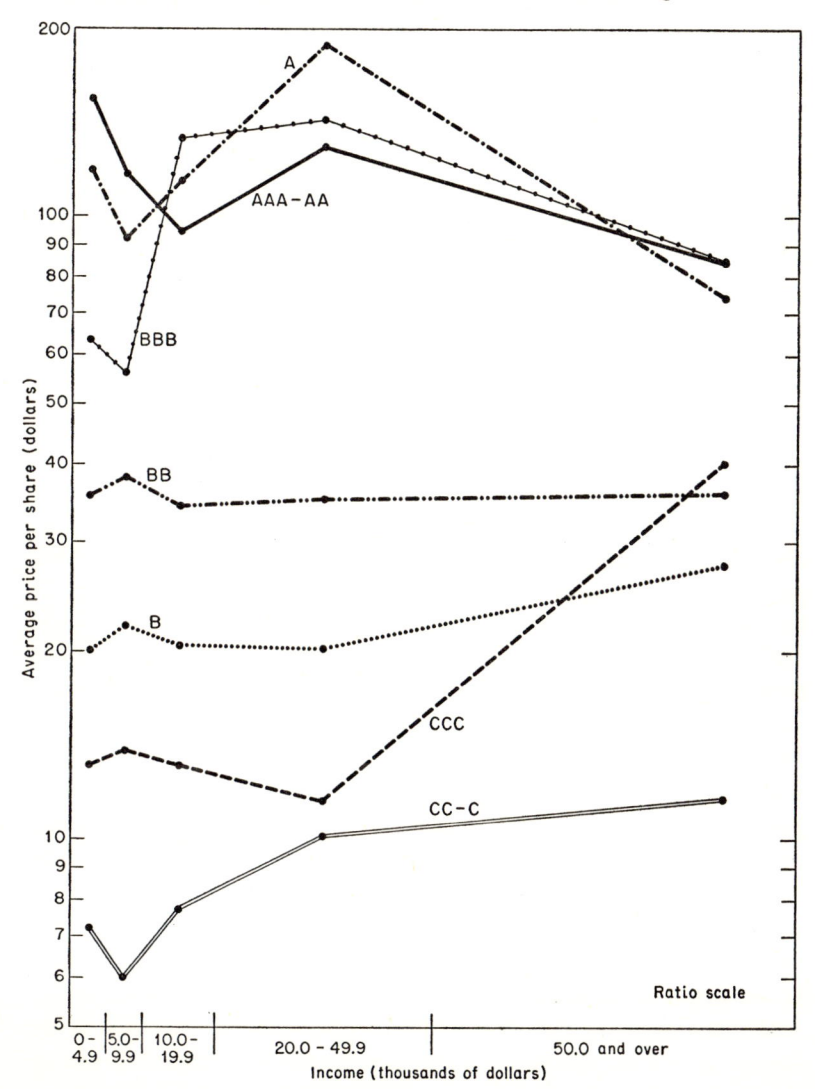

Based on survey of tax returns. Readings centered at midpoints of income class intervals, except that for the $50,000 and over class the approximate mean, $90,000, is used. Stocks are graded by Fitch agency rating as of December 1949.

to compound their speculative activities to a second degree. Whether this surmise is correct cannot be tested by present evidence.

137

TRADED STOCK HOLDINGS

Summary

The principal findings of the chapter are:

1. Income groups differ only slightly in the proportions of the dollar value of their traded stock consisting of issues traded on the New York Stock Exchange, the American Stock Exchange, and in over-the-counter and regional markets. Generally speaking, the proportion held in issues traded on the New York Stock Exchange is slightly higher for the low and middle income groups than for the upper income groups. But if "untraded" stocks are included among issues which find a market over the counter, the difference between income groups is considerably greater because of the concentration of untraded stock in the holdings of the higher income groups.

2. There is a significant shift, along the personal income scale, in the proportion of traded and of untraded stock holdings consisting of preferred as against common shares, with preferred issues considerably more important in the holdings of the lower than of higher income groups.

3. In general, the lower income group holds a greater proportion of the amount of its traded stock in issues of industries which are commonly regarded as conservative investments than the upper income groups do of theirs. Investment trust stock, issues of local utility companies, and American Telephone and Telegraph stock form a greater proportion of the holdings of the lower income group than of the higher income groups. On the other hand, stocks of pulp and paper, iron and steel, nonelectrical machinery, and trade concerns bulk larger in the higher than in the lower income groups. Petroleum stocks, generally regarded as relatively speculative, however, are an exception, being more important in lower than in higher income groups. In regard to untraded issues, bank stocks are important in the holdings of the lower and middle income groups while manufacturing stocks are of greatest importance in the upper income groups.

4. The average risk for different portfolios of issues bearing agency rating grades increases along the personal income scale by about two-fifths of one rating grade from the lowest income group (under $5,000) to the highest ($50,000 and over). Within each income group, however, individuals with small amounts of traded stock generally have more speculative positions than do those with larger holdings. One reason that the difference in risk between the

TRADED STOCK HOLDINGS

traded stock portfolios of the lowest and highest income groups is not greater appears to be the fact that the lower income group contains proportionately more small holders with relatively risky positions than the upper income groups.

5. The average number of issues held is greater, and the percentage of individuals holding only one issue is less, for groups with progressively higher incomes and with progressively larger individual holdings of traded stock.

6. The yield obtained in 1949 on traded stock holdings was slightly lower for progressively higher income groups up to the $50,000 level, but for the topmost income group ($50,000 and over) the yield exceeded the average for any other group. In contrast, the yield on untraded stock holdings was consistently larger the higher the income group.

7. Individuals with incomes of less than $50,000 had a slightly greater turnover in their traded stock holdings than did those in the highest income group. In addition, the stock sold by the lower income group had been held for a shorter length of time than that sold by the higher income groups.

8. The lower and middle income groups contained proportionately more individuals whose traded stock holdings had a low average price per share (under $20) than did the higher income groups. On the other hand, the lower and middle income groups contained a considerably greater proportion of individuals whose traded stock holdings had a high average price per share ($50 and over). It appears that low quality stocks held by the lower income group have a lower price per share than those held by the higher income groups. In the case of high quality stocks, however, the relationship is apparently reversed.

Appendix A

TABLE A-1

Estimated Amount of Interest and Dividend Income from Financial Asset Holdings of Wisconsin Individuals, by Income of Recipient and Type of Asset, 1949
(in thousands)

		INCOME OF RECIPIENT					
TYPE OF ASSET	Negative	$0-4,999	$5,000-9,999	$10,000-19,999	$20,000-49,999	$50,000 & Over	TOTAL
Time Deposits and Related Claims							
Commercial bank savings accounts	$51	$5,871	$1,849	$608	$248	$58	$8,685
Savings and loan association shares	26	2,836	686	211	131	26	3,916
Mutual savings bank deposits	25	2,630	1,058	380	110	29	4,232
Credit union shares	...	57	12	3	3	2	77
Postal savings deposits	...	182	75	9	a	1	267
	...	167	18	4	4	a	193
Direct Debt Assets							
Notes and mortgages—individuals	502	10,712	4,614	2,752	1,730	773	21,083
Notes and mortgages—business firms	323	8,144	2,637	1,466	653	260	13,483
State and local bonds	36	1,407	1,198	794	673	207	4,315
Corporate and other bonds	12	86	71	65	108	205	547
	131	1,075	708	427	296	101	2,738
Total Interest Receipts	553	16,583	6,463	3,360	1,978	831	29,768
Indirect debt assets	51	5,871	1,849	608	248	58	8,685
Direct debt assets	502	10,712	4,614	2,752	1,730	773	21,083
Corporate Stock	3,730	18,584	15,108	15,562	21,090	23,683	97,757
Traded stock	2,541	15,388	11,062	10,135	11,160	10,370	60,656
Untraded stock	1,189	3,196	4,046	5,427	9,930	13,313	37,100
Total Interest and Dividend Income	4,283	35,167	21,571	18,922	23,068	24,514	127,525
Interest receipts	553	16,583	6,463	3,360	1,978	831	29,768
Dividend receipts	3,730	18,584	15,108	15,562	21,090	23,683	97,757

Based on survey of tax returns. Detail will not always add to totals because of rounding.
a Less than $500.

APPENDIX A

TABLE A-2
Derivation of Market Value Equivalent for Untraded Stock Held by Income Groups of Wisconsin Individuals, 1949
(*in thousands*)

INCOME	BOOK VALUE Bank Stock	BOOK VALUE Nonbank Stock	BOOK VALUE Total	MARKET VALUE EQUIVALENT Bank Stock[a]	MARKET VALUE EQUIVALENT Nonbank Stock[b]	MARKET VALUE EQUIVALENT Total
Negative	$1,711	$14,650	$16,361	$1,489	$10,841	$12,330
$0-4,999	21,154	62,160	83,314	18,404	45,998	64,402
5,000-9,999	26,510	79,662	106,172	23,064	58,950	82,014
10,000-19,999	17,399	105,406	122,805	15,137	78,000	93,138
20,000-49,999	14,485	184,254	198,739	12,602	136,348	148,950
50,000 and over	7,506	249,996	257,502	6,530	184,997	191,527
All income groups	$88,765	$696,128	$784,893	$77,226	$515,134	$592,360

Based on survey of tax returns. Detail will not always add to totals because of rounding.

[a] Represents book value multiplied by 0.87, the ratio of book to market value in 1949 of twenty-one stocks of banks located outside New York City as computed from data in Standard and Poor's *Industry Surveys*.

[b] Represents book value multiplied by 0.74, the ratio of book to market value in 1949 of stocks of industrial and miscellaneous corporations as computed from "Estimate of Market Value of Corporate Stock: 1900-1949," by Raymond W. Goldsmith and Alexander Ganz (National Bureau of Economic Research, Capital Requirements Study, Work Memorandum 32, mimeographed, December 1951), Table 21, p. 64.

APPENDIX A

TABLE A-3
Estimated Value of Financial Asset Holdings of Wisconsin Individuals, by Income of Holder and Type of Asset, 1949
(in millions)

			INCOME OF HOLDER				
TYPE OF ASSET	Negative	$0–4,999	$5,000–9,999	$10,000–19,999	$20,000–49,999	$50,000 & Over	TOTAL
Time Deposits and Related Claims	$3.9	$444.7	$122.6	$39.0	$19.7	$4.2	$634.1
Commercial bank savings accounts	3.0	333.7	80.7	24.8	15.4	3.1	460.7
Savings and loan association shares	0.9	92.5	37.3	13.4	3.9	1.0	149.0
Mutual savings bank deposits	...	2.8	0.6	0.2	0.2	0.1	3.9
Credit union shares	...	7.4	3.1	0.4	a	a	10.9
Postal savings deposits	...	8.3	0.9	0.2	0.2	a	9.6
Direct Debt Assets	10.5	217.4	94.5	57.5	38.4	19.9	438.2
Notes and mortgages—individuals	6.5	162.9	52.7	29.3	13.1	5.2	269.7
Notes and mortgages—business firms	0.7	28.1	24.0	15.9	13.5	4.1	86.3
State and local bonds	0.4	3.2	2.8	2.2	4.6	8.2	21.5
Corporate and other bonds	2.9	23.2	15.0	10.1	7.2	2.3	60.8
Total Debt Assets	14.4	662.1	217.1	96.5	58.1	24.1	1,072.3
Indirect debt assets	3.9	444.7	122.6	39.0	19.7	4.2	634.1
Direct debt assets	10.5	217.4	94.5	57.5	38.4	19.9	438.2
Corporate Equity Assets	58.7	285.3	250.6	248.7	326.7	336.6	1,506.8
Traded stock[b]	46.4	220.9	168.6	155.6	177.8	145.1	914.4
Untraded stock[c]	12.3	64.4	82.0	93.1	148.9	191.5	592.4
Total Financial Assets	73.1	947.4	467.7	345.2	384.8	360.7	2,579.1
Debt assets	14.4	662.1	217.1	96.5	58.1	24.1	1,072.3
Corporate equity assets	58.7	285.3	250.6	248.7	326.7	336.6	1,506.8

Based on survey of tax returns. Detail will not always add to total because of rounding.
[a] Less than $50,000.
[b] Market value.
[c] Market value equivalent.

APPENDIX A

TABLE A-4

Estimated Value of Specified Types of Financial Asset Held by Wisconsin Individuals, and Estimated Number of Holders of Some Such Asset, by Size of Holdings and Income of Holder, 1949

(dollar figures in millions)

INCOME OF HOLDER AND TYPE OF ASSET	Less than $10,000	$10,000-19,999	$20,000-99,999	$100,000-999,999	$1,000,000 and Over	TOTAL
Negative						
Time deposits & rel. claims	$2.7	$3.4	$8.6	$62.7	...	$77.2
Direct debt	0.5	0.6	2.8	0.1	...	3.9
Traded stock	0.4	0.6	5.6	4.0	...	10.5
Untraded stock[a]	1.0	0.9	0.2	44.4	...	46.4
	0.8	1.3	...	14.2	...	16.4
Number of holders (000)	0.8	0.3	0.2	0.1	...	1.4
$0-4,999						
Time deposits & rel. claims	388.0	224.4	353.8	...	...	966.3
Direct debt	240.0	103.1	101.6	...	...	444.7
Traded stock	75.9	50.5	90.9	...	...	217.4
Untraded stock[a]	49.2	48.6	123.2	...	...	220.9
	22.9	22.2	38.1	...	...	83.3
Number of holders (000)	129.4	16.3	10.4	...	...	156.1
$5,000-9,999						
Time deposits & rel. claims	81.4	69.7	234.4	106.2	...	491.9
Direct debt	41.1	28.0	40.7	12.7	...	122.6
Traded stock	14.2	11.8	42.3	26.1	...	94.5
Untraded stock[a]	17.5	14.7	93.8	42.6	...	168.6
	8.6	15.2	57.6	24.8	...	106.2
Number of holders (000)	24.0	5.1	5.9	0.8	...	35.7
$10,000-19,999						
Time deposits & rel. claims	18.8	25.1	176.1	154.8	...	374.9
Direct debt	4.8	6.7	23.8	3.8	...	39.0
Traded stock	3.7	3.1	27.3	23.3	...	57.5
Untraded stock[a]	7.2	9.7	65.0	73.6	...	155.6
	3.1	5.6	60.0	54.1	...	122.8
Number of holders (000)	5.1	1.7	3.7	0.9	...	11.5

(continued on next page)

TABLE A-4 (continued)
(dollar figures in millions)

INCOME OF HOLDER AND TYPE OF ASSET	Less than $10,000	$10,000-19,999	$20,000-99,999	$100,000-999,999	$1,000,000 and Over	TOTAL
$20,000-49,999						
Time deposits & rel. claims	$3.6	$6.6	$87.1	$326.3	$10.8	$434.7
Direct debt	0.8	1.3	9.0	8.4	...	19.7
Traded stock	0.8	1.4	10.9	25.2	0.1	38.4
Untraded stock[a]	1.5	2.2	30.6	142.5	0.9	177.8
	0.5	1.7	36.6	150.2	9.8	198.8
Number of holders (000)	0.8	0.4	1.8	1.2	[b]	4.3
$50,000 and Over						
Time deposits & rel. claims	0.1	0.3	7.2	148.5	270.4	426.6
Direct debt	...	...	1.0	2.1	0.9	4.2
Traded stock	...	0.1	1.1	10.5	8.2	19.9
Untraded stock[a]	0.1	0.1	2.8	45.0	97.1	145.1
	...	0.1	2.3	90.9	164.2	257.4
Number of holders (000)	[b]	[b]	0.1	0.4	0.1	0.7
All Income Groups						
Time deposits & rel. claims	494.5	329.5	867.2	798.5	281.2	2,771.6
Direct debt	287.2	139.7	178.9	27.1	0.9	634.1
Traded stock	95.0	67.5	178.1	89.1	8.3	438.2
Untraded stock[a]	76.5	76.2	315.6	348.1	98.0	914.4
	35.8	46.1	194.6	334.2	174.0	784.9
Number of holders (000)	160.1	23.8	22.1	3.4	0.1	209.7

Based on survey of tax returns. Detail will not always add to totals because of rounding.
[a] Book value.
[b] Less than 50 holders.

APPENDIX A

TABLE A-5
Estimated Number of Wisconsin Individuals Holding
Specified Types of Financial Asset, by Income of Holder, 1949
(in thousands)

Income of Holder	Some Financial Asset[a]	Time Deposits & Related Claims	Direct Debt Assets	Traded Stock	Untraded Stock	Some Corporate Stock[b]
Negative	1.4	0.8	0.5	0.7	0.7	0.9
$0-4,999	156.1	107.6	47.5	44.2	25.6	58.1
5,000-9,999	35.7	20.7	11.3	15.9	11.0	20.4
10,000-19,999	11.5	4.8	4.4	7.4	5.4	9.3
20,000-49,999	4.3	1.6	2.0	3.1	2.8	3.9
50,000 and over	0.7	0.3	0.4	0.6	0.6	0.7
Total	209.7	135.7	66.2	72.0	46.2	93.3

Based on survey of tax returns. Detail will not always add to totals because of rounding.

[a] The number of individuals holding some financial asset of the types specified is less than the sum of the number of holders for all types because some individuals held more than one type.

[b] The number of individuals holding some corporate stock is less than the sum of the number of holders of traded and untraded stock because some individuals held stock of both types.

APPENDIX A

TABLE A-6
Estimated Mean and Median Size of Holdings for Specified Types of Financial Asset Held by Wisconsin Individuals, 1949, by Income of Holder

| TYPE OF ASSET AND | SIZE OF HOLDINGS | |
INCOME OF HOLDER	Mean	Median
Time Deposits & Rel. Claims	$4,670	$3,219
Negative	5,179	2,503
$0-4,999	4,133	3,043
5,000-9,999	5,907	3,801
10,000-19,999	8,223	4,754
20,000-49,999	12,155	6,306
50,000 and over	15,087	7,193
Direct Debt Assets	6,617	3,366
Negative	20,897	20,120
$0-4,999	4,576	3,067
5,000-9,999	8,354	3,791
10,000-19,999	12,905	4,744
20,000-49,999	18,940	6,737
50,000 and over	47,354	19,531
Traded Stock	12,700	2,971
Negative	68,770	4,000
$0-4,999	4,997	2,008
5,000-9,999	10,591	3,876
10,000-19,999	20,828	6,020
20,000-49,999	56,676	17,679
50,000 and over	245,184	51,280
Untraded Stock[a]	16,993	2,867
Negative	24,239	2,344
$0-4,999	3,250	1,438
5,000-9,999	9,670	1,646
10,000-19,999	22,414	8,881
20,000-49,999	70,550	29,309
50,000 and over	425,623	251,020

Based on survey of tax returns.
[a] Represents book value.

TABLE A-7

Estimated Number of Wisconsin Individuals Holding Specified Types of Financial Asset, by Occupation and Income of Holder, 1949

(*in thousands*)

TYPE OF ASSET AND INCOME OF HOLDER	Professional	Managerial and Self-Employed	Clerical & Sales	Skilled & Semi-skilled	Unskilled	Farm Operators	House-wives, etc.	Retired	All Others & Un-specified	TOTAL
Time Dep., Rel. Claims	12.9	14.2	21.7	32.6	25.1	12.8	3.6	5.4	7.6	135.7
Negative	0.1	0.1	...	...	...	0.3	0.2	0.1	0.1	0.8
$0-4,999	7.4	5.4	18.6	27.0	23.8	11.7	2.9	4.5	6.4	107.6
5,000-9,999	3.6	5.3	2.6	5.4	1.3	0.8	0.4	0.6	0.8	20.7
10,000 and over	1.8	3.4	0.5	0.2	a	a	0.1	0.2	0.3	6.6
Direct Debt	6.2	11.7	5.7	7.5	8.2	9.5	3.4	6.4	7.5	66.2
Negative	0.1	a	...	...	...	0.2	...	0.1	0.2	0.5
$0-4,999	2.6	4.2	4.3	6.5	7.7	8.6	2.8	5.3	5.5	47.5
5,000-9,999	2.1	3.8	0.9	0.9	0.5	0.7	0.4	0.8	1.2	11.3
10,000 and over	1.4	3.7	0.5	0.1	a	a	0.2	0.2	0.6	6.9
Traded Stock	13.4	14.3	10.4	10.3	5.3	2.8	3.6	5.2	6.5	72.0
Negative	0.1	0.1	...	...	...	0.1	0.1	0.2	0.2	0.7
$0-4,999	5.8	3.4	7.9	8.4	5.1	2.3	2.6	4.1	4.4	44.2
5,000-9,999	4.7	4.9	1.7	1.7	0.2	0.4	0.6	0.6	1.0	15.9
10,000 and over	2.8	5.9	0.8	0.2	a	a	0.3	0.3	0.9	11.2
Untraded Stock	5.9	12.8	4.8	5.2	3.0	4.6	2.3	3.5	4.3	46.2
Negative	0.1	0.2	...	...	...	0.2	0.1	0.1	0.1	0.7
$0-4,999	1.9	3.1	3.1	4.1	2.9	3.8	1.7	2.7	2.4	25.6
5,000-9,999	2.1	4.4	1.0	0.9	0.1	0.5	0.3	0.5	1.1	11.0
10,000 and over	1.8	5.1	0.7	0.2	a	0.1	0.2	0.2	0.7	8.9

Based on survey of tax returns. Detail will not always add to totals because of rounding. Returns of husband and wife both reporting income were put on a joint basis if not already so (here as throughout); occupational group in such cases is that of the head of the unit.

a Less than 50 individuals.

TABLE A-8

Estimated Value of Specified Types of Financial Asset Holdings of
Wisconsin Individuals, by Occupation and Income of Holder, 1949

(in millions)

INCOME OF HOLDER AND TYPE OF ASSET	Professional	Managerial and Self-Employed	Clerical & Sales	Skilled & Semi-skilled	Unskilled	Farm Operators	Housewives, etc.	Retired	All Others & Un-specified	TOTAL
Negative										
Time dep., etc.	$1.2	$1.4	...	...	...	$5.3	$1.4	$4.1	$59.7	$73.1
Direct debt	0.2	a	...	...	...	2.3	0.7	0.4	0.1	3.9
Direct debt	0.6	...	...	...	...	2.8	...	3.0	4.2	10.5
Traded stock	0.2	0.1	...	...	...	0.1	0.7	0.4	44.9	46.4
Untraded stock	0.2	1.3	...	...	...	0.1	...	0.3	10.5	12.3
$0-4,999										
Time dep., etc.	48.3	59.2	$99.0	$139.0	$136.3	135.5	68.2	142.2	119.8	947.4
Time dep., etc.	18.7	30.4	54.8	89.1	80.6	84.2	12.7	41.2	33.0	444.7
Direct debt	6.1	14.7	11.2	19.9	34.3	34.2	13.1	50.9	32.9	217.4
Traded stock	18.9	7.5	23.8	25.0	15.1	12.1	38.1	36.2	44.2	220.9
Untraded stock	4.6	6.5	9.1	5.0	6.3	4.9	4.2	13.9	9.7	64.4
$5,000-9,999										
Time dep., etc.	65.3	129.4	39.5	41.4	14.1	24.4	47.9	57.8	47.7	467.7
Time dep., etc.	17.4	26.4	13.9	26.4	5.2	8.9	3.7	15.5	5.0	122.6
Direct debt	8.0	31.2	4.6	2.4	6.9	8.1	7.0	17.2	9.1	94.5
Traded stock	30.7	34.4	14.7	9.1	0.9	4.7	36.4	18.7	18.9	168.6
Untraded stock	9.2	37.4	6.2	3.6	1.0	2.8	0.8	6.3	14.7	82.0
$10,000-19,999										
Time dep., etc.	72.5	146.6	24.0	5.7	0.3	0.9	28.5	23.6	43.1	345.2
Time dep., etc.	11.2	18.5	3.4	0.7	0.3	...	2.0	1.8	1.1	39.0
Direct debt	11.4	23.4	4.0	1.4	a	0.4	2.3	6.4	8.2	57.5
Traded stock	36.1	54.3	11.0	0.5	...	0.2	17.2	13.2	23.0	155.6
Untraded stock	13.8	50.4	5.6	3.1	a	0.3	7.0	2.2	10.8	93.1

(continued on next page)

TABLE A-8 (continued)

(in millions)

INCOME OF HOLDER AND TYPE OF ASSET	Professional	Managerial and Self-Employed	Clerical & Sales	Skilled & Semi-skilled	Unskilled	Farm Operators	Housewives, etc.	Retired	All Others & Unspecified	TOTAL
$20,000-49,999	$29.8	$219.7	$14.1	$0.6	$0.1	$2.0	$33.8	$37.0	$47.4	$384.8
Time dep., etc.	3.6	11.9	0.7	0.3	a	0.1	0.7	0.4	1.8	19.7
Direct debt	2.9	23.3	0.6	a	0.1	1.9	4.0	1.0	4.5	38.4
Traded stock	17.6	83.1	11.1	a	a	...	19.7	22.8	23.3	177.8
Untraded stock	5.6	101.3	1.7	0.3	...	...	9.3	12.8	17.9	148.9
$50,000 and Over	16.5	292.7	3.4	0.1	...	...	11.2	5.1	31.9	360.7
Time dep., etc.	0.4	3.3	0.1	a	a	...	0.1	...	0.3	4.2
Direct debt	1.0	14.0	0.5	a	...	...	0.8	0.3	3.4	19.9
Traded stock	6.5	108.4	0.9	a	...	...	7.9	3.0	18.5	145.1
Untraded stock	8.6	167.0	1.9	a	...	...	2.4	1.8	9.7	191.5
All Income Groups	233.6	848.9	180.0	186.9	150.8	168.1	191.1	269.8	349.7	2,579.1
Time dep., etc.	51.5	90.6	73.0	116.5	86.1	95.6	19.9	59.4	41.3	634.1
Direct debt	30.0	106.6	20.8	23.8	41.4	47.4	27.2	78.8	62.3	438.2
Traded stock	110.0	287.9	61.6	34.7	16.0	17.1	120.1	94.2	172.7	914.4
Untraded stock	42.1	363.8	24.5	11.9	7.4	8.0	23.9	37.4	73.3	592.4

Based on survey of tax returns. Detail will not always add to totals because of rounding. Returns of husband and wife both reporting income were put on a joint basis if not already so (here as throughout); occupational group in such cases is that of the head of the unit.
a Less than $50,000.

APPENDIX A

TABLE A-9

Estimated Number of Wisconsin Individuals Holding Specified Types of Financial Asset, by Size of Community and Income of Holder, 1949
(in thousands)

TYPE OF ASSET AND INCOME OF HOLDER	Less than 2,500[a]	2,500-9,999	10,000-24,999	25,000-49,999	50,000-149,999	Metropolitan[b]	TOTAL
Time Dep., etc.	31.1	13.1	7.0	20.1	24.7	39.6	135.7
Negative	0.5	0.1	...	0.2	...	...	0.8
$0-4,999	27.3	11.0	5.6	16.7	18.4	28.5	107.6
5,000-9,999	2.8	1.4	1.0	2.4	5.2	7.9	20.7
10,000 and over	0.5	0.6	0.4	0.8	1.1	3.2	6.6
Direct Debt	23.4	7.7	3.5	7.3	9.4	15.2	66.3
Negative	0.3	0.1	...	0.2	...	...	0.6
$0-4,999	20.0	5.6	2.4	5.2	6.0	8.3	47.5
5,000-9,999	2.4	1.1	0.7	1.2	2.2	3.8	11.3
10,000 and over	0.7	0.9	0.4	0.7	1.2	3.1	6.9
Traded Stock	12.1	7.1	3.7	10.4	13.0	25.7	72.0
Negative	0.2	0.1	...	0.3	...	0.1	0.7
$0-4,999	9.2	4.8	2.1	6.9	8.2	12.9	44.2
5,000-9,999	1.9	1.2	0.9	2.0	2.9	7.1	15.9
10,000 and over	0.8	1.0	0.7	1.2	1.9	5.6	11.2
Untraded Stock	12.7	4.9	2.9	6.5	7.3	11.8	46.2
Negative	0.3	0.1	...	0.2	0.1	...	0.7
$0-4,999	9.4	3.1	1.2	3.8	3.6	4.5	25.6
5,000-9,999	2.2	0.8	1.1	1.6	1.9	3.4	11.0
10,000 and over	0.8	0.9	0.6	0.9	1.7	3.9	8.9

Based on survey of tax returns. Detail will not always add to totals because of rounding.
[a] Includes rural areas.
[b] Includes Milwaukee county and adjoining residential areas in southern Ozaukee county.

TABLE A-10

Estimated Value of Specified Types of Financial Asset Holdings of Wisconsin Individuals, by Size of Community and Income of Holder, 1949

(in millions)

INCOME OF HOLDER AND TYPE OF ASSET	Less than 2,500[a]	2,500-9,999	10,000-24,999	SIZE OF COMMUNITY 25,000-49,999	50,000-149,999	Metropolitan[b]	TOTAL
Negative	$7.3	$1.2	...	$63.1	$1.0	$0.6	$73.1
Time dep., etc.	3.1	0.2	...	0.6	...	...	3.9
Direct debt	3.0	0.6	...	7.0	...	...	10.5
Traded Stock	0.9	0.2	...	44.7	...	0.6	46.4
Untraded stock	0.3	0.2	...	10.8	1.0	...	12.3
$0-4,999	320.6	112.5	$47.1	103.4	149.6	214.2	947.4
Time dep., etc.	167.5	46.4	14.9	51.3	62.2	102.4	444.7
Direct debt	95.7	26.4	18.1	16.4	26.0	34.9	217.4
Traded Stock	40.4	33.8	6.7	28.9	48.7	62.4	220.9
Untraded stock	17.0	5.9	7.4	6.8	12.7	14.5	64.4
$5,000-9,999	99.3	22.5	42.3	66.8	84.4	152.2	467.7
Time dep., etc.	27.9	5.3	4.2	15.9	28.7	40.4	122.6
Direct debt	21.0	4.4	15.2	5.6	19.6	28.7	94.5
Traded Stock	27.5	6.0	13.2	30.1	21.3	70.4	168.6
Untraded stock	22.9	6.8	9.7	15.2	14.8	12.7	82.0
$10,000-19,999	28.4	40.4	24.7	43.8	49.0	158.8	345.2
Time dep., etc.	2.7	4.9	3.2	5.4	5.4	17.5	39.0
Direct debt	6.6	10.0	4.9	6.0	4.4	25.5	57.5
Traded Stock	7.5	12.3	12.5	19.2	23.9	80.0	155.6
Untraded stock	11.6	13.2	4.1	13.2	15.3	35.8	93.1

(continued on next page)

APPENDIX A

TABLE A-10 (continued)
(in millions)

INCOME OF HOLDER AND TYPE OF ASSET	Less than 2,500[a]	2,500- 9,999	SIZE OF COMMUNITY 10,000- 24,999	25,000- 49,999	50,000- 149,999	Metropolitan[b]	TOTAL
$20,000-49,999	$34.4	$33.1	$35.5	$33.4	$83.3	$164.8	$384.8
Time dep., etc.	2.8	1.4	1.3	1.9	3.6	8.5	19.7
Direct debt	6.5	2.1	1.6	3.3	7.0	17.8	38.4
Traded Stock	15.8	12.5	22.7	15.6	33.4	77.8	177.8
Untraded stock	9.3	17.1	9.9	12.6	39.3	60.7	148.9
$50,000 and Over	17.5	23.4	24.8	77.1	78.4	139.3	360.7
Time dep., etc.	0.3	0.4	0.3	0.9	0.7	1.6	4.2
Direct debt	1.0	1.3	2.3	3.9	3.0	8.4	19.9
Traded Stock	4.8	7.3	8.7	30.4	26.7	67.1	145.1
Untraded stock	11.4	14.4	13.5	41.9	48.0	62.2	191.5
All Income Groups	507.7	233.2	174.5	387.4	445.8	830.2	2,579.1
Time dep., etc.	204.2	58.6	23.9	75.9	100.7	170.5	634.1
Direct debt	133.8	44.8	42.1	42.2	59.9	115.4	438.2
Traded Stock	97.2	72.1	63.8	168.9	154.1	358.3	914.4
Untraded stock	72.5	57.7	44.7	100.4	131.1	186.0	592.4

Based on survey of tax returns. Detail will not always add to totals because of rounding.
[a] Includes rural areas.
[b] Includes Milwaukee county and adjoining residential areas in southern Ozaukee county.

APPENDIX A

TABLE A-11
Estimated Dividends from Traded and from Untraded Stocks, and
Value of Holdings, for Income Groups of Wisconsin Individuals, 1949

INCOME	DIVIDENDS (THOUSANDS) Preferred	Common	Total	VALUE (MILLIONS)[a] Preferred	Common	Total
			Traded Stock			
Negative	$261	$2,281	$2,541	$5.9	$40.5	$46.4
$0-4,999	1,669	13,719	15,388	32.5	188.4	220.9
5,000-9,999	1,084	9,978	11,062	22.6	146.0	168.6
10,000-19,999	820	9,315	10,135	16.6	139.0	155.6
20,000-49,999	862	10,298	11,160	18.7	159.1	177.8
50,000 and over	356	10,014	10,370	8.2	137.0	145.1
All income groups	$5,052	$55,604	$60,656	$104.4	$809.9	$914.4
			Untraded Stock[b]			
Negative	...	$1,162	$1,162	...	$15.8	$15.8
$0-4,999	$412	1,545	1,957	$10.5	48.1	58.6
5,000-9,999	559	2,409	2,968	7.4	77.6	85.1
10,000-19,999	468	3,998	4,466	9.2	93.8	103.1
20,000-49,999	586	7,957	8,543	10.3	161.7	172.0
50,000 and over	349	10,457	10,806	5.7	205.2	210.9
All income groups	$2,373	$27,527	$29,901	$43.2	$602.3	$645.5

Based on survey of tax returns. Detail will not always add to totals because of rounding.
[a] Represents market value of traded stock and unadjusted book value of untraded stock.
[b] Includes identifiable issues only.

APPENDIX A

TABLE A-12
Industrial Classification of Traded Stock Holdings of Wisconsin Individuals, by Income of Holder, 1949
(in millions)

			INCOME OF HOLDER			
INDUSTRIAL CLASSIFICATION	Negative	$0-4,999	$5,000-9,999	$10,000-19,999	$20,000-49,999	$50,000 & Over	TOTAL
Mining (except oil and gas)	$0.3	$2.0	$4.9	$3.3	$4.3	$2.2	$17.0
Oil and gas extraction and manufacturing	0.9	15.5	8.4	7.8	10.2	5.8	48.6
Food and tobacco manufacturing	2.5	13.7	7.0	10.0	8.6	7.7	49.5
Textiles and apparel	1.7	2.3	1.3	2.8	5.9	4.7	18.7
Wood and wood products (except paper)	0.5	7.6	5.1	1.7	8.4	5.2	28.5
Pulp and paper	0.8	12.7	8.5	12.7	17.8	12.0	64.5
Chemicals	4.6	5.8	13.8	7.3	11.3	6.4	49.2
Iron and steel	0.7	9.3	9.8	8.4	16.0	11.0	55.2
Nonferrous metals	1.2	4.4	1.0	1.9	2.6	8.0	19.1
Machinery (except electrical)	0.6	8.3	5.7	9.7	10.0	13.0	47.3
Electrical machinery	0.5	8.4	10.1	6.1	6.2	5.5	36.8
Transport equipment (except autos)	1.3	3.2	3.3	1.8	5.7	1.3	16.6
Automobiles and equipment	0.6	17.9	12.9	10.2	11.8	15.8	69.2
All other manufacturing	0.5	7.7	6.9	4.1	4.2	8.9	32.3
Wholesale and retail trade	0.3	5.3	6.0	4.4	8.5	10.9	35.4
Banks	12.1	7.7	9.7	11.6	12.1	6.4	59.6

(continued on next page)

TABLE A-12 (continued)
(in millions)

INDUSTRIAL CLASSIFICATION	Negative	$0-4,999	$5,000-9,999	$10,000-19,999	$20,000-49,999	$50,000 & Over	TOTAL
Closed-end investment trusts	...	2.2	0.5	0.8	0.7	1.2	5.4
Open-end investment trusts	3.3	16.8	7.4	9.3	7.7	2.8	47.3
All other finance	0.8	7.3	3.4	7.1	4.7	2.6	25.9
Transportation	0.5	5.9	4.2	3.9	3.3	1.6	19.4
Electric and gas utilities in Wisconsin	0.6	16.9	7.4	9.1	3.5	2.4	39.9
Other electric and gas utilities	9.8	10.5	19.0	13.1	11.4	8.6	72.4
American Telephone and Telegraph	0.4	16.5	9.0	5.7	1.8	0.7	34.1
All others	1.9	13.0	3.3	2.8	1.1	0.4	22.5
Total	$46.4	$220.9	$168.6	$155.6	$177.8	$145.1	$914.4

Based on survey of tax returns. Detail will not always add to totals because of rounding.

APPENDIX A

TABLE A-13
Industrial Classification of Untraded Stock Holdings of Wisconsin Individuals, by Income of Holder, 1949
(*in millions*)

INDUSTRIAL CLASSIFICATION	Negative	$0-4,999	$5,000-9,999	$10,000-19,999	$20,000-49,999	$50,000 & Over	TOTAL
Construction	...	...	$0.3	$1.1	$3.5	$3.1	$8.0
Manufacturing	$1.1	$15.2	18.1	41.7	73.0	122.9	271.9
Wholesale and retail trade	9.1	3.4	16.0	12.6	24.1	6.9	72.1
Banking	1.5	18.4	23.1	15.1	12.6	6.5	77.2
Transportation, communication, and public utility	0.3	0.9	0.4	1.8	3.4	1.0	7.8
Services (except trade)	...	0.5	3.4	0.1	1.3	0.6	6.0
All others	...	7.6	5.1	6.1	11.3	16.4	46.5
Total	$12.0	$46.0	$66.4	$78.5	$129.2	$157.4	$489.5

Based on survey of tax returns and includes market value equivalent of identifiable issues only. Detail will not always add to totals because of rounding.

TABLE A-14

Estimated Value of Rated Stock Holdings of Wisconsin Individuals, by Income of Holder and Grade of Stock, 1949
(in millions)

FITCH AGENCY RATING DECEMBER 1949	Negative	$0-4,999	$5,000-9,999	$10,000-19,999	$20,000-49,999	$50,000 & Over	TOTAL
AAA	...	$0.2	$0.9	$0.2	$0.4	$0.2	$1.9
AA	$0.3	0.1	1.4	0.7	0.6	0.2	3.2
A	3.1	21.2	14.4	10.1	9.6	2.9	61.2
BBB	4.7	24.9	17.3	12.6	15.9	8.9	84.4
BB	13.5	55.6	46.2	40.5	51.2	44.5	251.5
B	4.5	41.5	31.3	34.4	29.2	39.5	180.3
CCC	2.5	17.5	12.0	9.6	11.7	20.2	73.4
CC	1.6	10.2	8.7	3.0	6.0	1.5	31.0
C	...	0.1	0.5	0.6	3.3	1.0	5.5
Total	$30.0	$171.3	$132.7	$111.8	$128.0	$118.9	$692.6

Based on survey of tax returns. Detail will not always add to totals because of rounding.

APPENDIX A

TABLE A-15

Risk Position of Wisconsin Individuals Holding Rated Stock, by Income of Holder, 1949

INCOME OF HOLDER	NUMBER OF INDIVIDUALS WHOSE HOLDINGS HAD AN AVERAGE FITCH AGENCY RATING OF:					TOTAL
	AAA-A	BBB	BB	B	CCC-C	
Negative	...	170	250	250	...	670
$0-4,999	4,000	8,270	11,560	9,960	5,510	39,300
5,000-9,999	1,440	2,210	4,720	4,100	2,120	14,590
10,000-19,999	280	1,060	3,130	1,660	800	6,930
20,000-49,999	110	510	1,260	710	280	2,870
50,000 and over	20	120	250	120	50	560
All income levels	5,850	12,340	21,170	16,800	8,760	64,920

Based on survey of tax returns. For method of calculating risk position, see pages 119 ff. Ratings are those of December 1949. Detail will not always add to totals because of rounding.

TABLE A-16

Estimated Value of Traded Stock Sold by Wisconsin Individuals, by Income of Holder and Length of Time Held, 1949
(in millions)

			INCOME OF HOLDER			
LENGTH OF TIME HELD	*Negative*	*$0-4,999*	*$5,000-9,999*	*$10,000-19,999*	*$20,000-49,999*	*$50,000 & Over*	TOTAL
6 months and under	...	$2.5	$1.9	$1.2	$2.5	$0.3	$8.4
6 months to 1 year	...	3.5	3.5	2.0	1.4	0.7	11.0
1 to 2 years	...	4.3	2.8	4.7	2.5	1.4	15.7
2 to 5 years	$1.4	2.3	1.6	2.6	2.3	1.4	11.6
5 to 10 years	...	0.6	0.9	1.0	1.8	0.8	5.2
Over 10 years	0.4	0.2	2.1	1.0	0.9	0.6	5.2
Indeterminate	...	1.2	1.5	0.1	0.8	0.7	4.3
Total	$1.8	$14.6	$14.3	$12.6	$12.2	$5.9	$61.3

Based on survey of tax returns. Detail will not always add to totals because of rounding.

APPENDIX A

TABLE A-17
Estimated Distribution of Wisconsin Individuals Holding Traded Stock, by Average Price per Share Held and Income of Holder, 1949

	NUMBER OF INDIVIDUALS WHOSE HOLDINGS HAD AN AVERAGE PRICE PER SHARE OF:							
INCOME OF HOLDER	$0-4.99	$5.00-9.99	$10.00-19.99	$20.00-29.99	$30.00-39.99	$40.00-49.99	$50.00-99.99	$100.00 & Over	TOTAL
Negative	...	...	170	80	80	170	170	...	670
$0-4,999	940	3,170	12,960	10,410	4,040	3,250	4,360	5,080	44,200
5,000-9,999	180	1,240	5,280	3,630	2,580	830	830	1,340	15,900
10,000-19,999	80	350	2,380	2,720	810	390	390	340	7,460
20,000-49,999	70	180	1,020	1,000	460	160	190	30	3,120
50,000 and over	10	20	160	220	100	40	20	20	590
All income groups	1,290	4,950	21,960	18,070	8,070	4,830	5,950	6,810	71,940

Based on survey of tax returns. Detail will not always add to totals because of rounding.